IMPHAL KOHIMA 1944

INDIA'S HISTORIC BATTLES:
A SERIES

IMPHAL KOHIMA 1944

HEMANT SINGH KATOCH

SERIES EDITED BY
SQN LDR RANA CHHINA (RETD)

HarperCollins *Publishers* India

First published in India by HarperCollins *Publishers* 2024
4th Floor, Tower A, Building No. 10, DLF Cyber City,
DLF Phase II, Gurugram, Haryana – 122002
www.harpercollins.co.in

In collaboration with the United Service Institution of India

2 4 6 8 10 9 7 5 3 1

Copyright © Hemant Singh Katoch 2024
Contributing photographer: Findlay Kember

P-ISBN: 978-93-5489-912-6
E-ISBN: 978-93-5489-958-4

The views and opinions expressed in this book are the author's own. The facts are as reported by him and the publishers are not in any way liable for the same.

Hemant Singh Katoch asserts the moral right
to be identified as the author of this work.

All rights reserved. No part of this publication may be reproduced, stored in a retrieval system, or transmitted, in any form or by any means, electronic, mechanical, photocopying, recording or otherwise, without the prior permission of the publishers.

Typeset in 11.5/15.5 Adobe Garamond at
Manipal Technologies Limited, Manipal

Printed and bound at
Thomson Press (India) Ltd.

This book is produced from independently certified FSC® paper
to ensure responsible forest management.

Contents

Preface	ix
Setting the Stage	1
The Warring Sides	14
Chronology of Events	33
Battle Sites	39
IMPHAL	43
Imphal	46
The Tiddim Road and the Silchar–Bishenpur Track	51
The Tamu–Palel Road and the Shenam Saddle	80
The Ukhrul Road and the Iril River Valley	95
The Mapao–Molvom Range and the Imphal–Kohima Road	113
KOHIMA	129
Kohima Ridge	135
Kohima War Cemetery	146

Aradura Spur and GPT Ridge	149
Naga Village	156
Merema Ridge	159
Kisama, Kigwema and the Road to Imphal	160
Jotsoma	163
Zubza	165
Dimapur	166
LEDO ROAD AND THE HUMP	**169**
Dibrugarh and Chabua	172
Digboi	174
Ledo Airfield	175
Zero Point	176
Lekhapani Railway Station	178
Arunachal Pradesh: Jairampur, Pangsau Pass and Pasighat	181
Practical Information for Visitors	187
Acknowledgements	191
Bibliography	193
Index	195

Maps

Northeast India	xi
The Battle of Imphal	42
The Tiddim Road and the Silchar–Bishenpur Track	50
The Tamu–Palel Road and the Shenam Saddle	79
The Ukhrul Road, the Iril River Valley and the Imphal–Kohima Road	94
Kohima battlefield locations	128
Allied lines of communication in India, Burma and China in 1942–43	168

Preface

THE CLASH BETWEEN THE BRITISH Fourteenth Army and the Japanese Fifteenth Army at Imphal in Manipur and at Kohima in the Naga Hills of what was then Assam in 1944 was the turning point in the Burma Campaign of the Second World War. It was at these twin battles that the Japanese invasion of India and march through Asia was stopped, with the Allies subsequently driving them out of Burma (Myanmar today) in 1945. The Japanese lost some 30,000 men, with another 23,000 injured, in what is considered one of their greatest-ever defeats on land. In April 2013, Imphal–Kohima was named 'Britain's Greatest Battle' by the UK's National Army Museum. Indians fought on both sides—as part of the Fourteenth Army and, albeit in much smaller numbers, alongside the Japanese as soldiers of the Indian National Army (INA).

This book is the first battlefield guide for Imphal and Kohima. It looks at what the present-day states of Manipur and Nagaland have to offer about the two battles and the Second World War, including battlefields, memorials, airfields, cemeteries and museums. In the process, it describes the forces that clashed at the time, their strategies and the bitter fighting that ensued. The guide also briefly presents sites of interest in Assam and Arunachal Pradesh that are linked to the war-era Ledo/Stillwell Road and flights over the 'Hump'.

The text is supported by maps and, especially, present-day images of the Second World War sites in Northeast India. Many of these have been taken by Findlay Kember, who made a series of journeys travelling the length of the Ledo/Stillwell Road, and has also extensively travelled Manipur and Nagaland. We consider the use of these images important for they bring to life and reveal the immensely rich Second World War heritage of the region. It is a heritage that has remained forgotten for far too long. As Northeast India becomes more accessible, these sites deserve to be visited, their history remembered, and their future secured through upkeep and preservation.

Findlay's photos have been combined with the many pictures I have taken in the course of my stay, work and travel in Northeast India in connection with the Second World War. I lived in Manipur for just under three years, from 2012 to 2014. I conceived of the original idea to commemorate the 70th anniversary of the Imphal battle and helped organize it in 2014. I also made the first public call for the establishment of a proper museum dedicated to this battle and Manipur's experience of the war. I further researched, designed and launched the first battlefield tours around Imphal, subsequently expanding them to Kohima, the rest of Northeast India, and finally Burma.

It should be noted that this book is not intended to be an exhaustive military history of the twin battles of Imphal and Kohima and the events farther north. Instead, it should be used as an adjunct to the many excellent accounts that have been written about them. Finally, research into and promotion of the battlefields and other reminders of the Second World War in Northeast India is still at a relatively nascent stage and remains a work in progress. Many battlefields are still being mapped and remains of bunkers and trenches, as well as relics of war, continue to be discovered on a regular basis; newer war-related memorials are also being erected and personal museums being established. Through this battlefield guide, we hope to assist that process along and contribute to increasing awareness about this fascinating chapter of history.

Northeast India

1
Setting the Stage

'The Imphal plain, some forty by twenty miles in extent, is the only considerable oasis of flat ground in the great sweep of mountains between India and Burma. It lies roughly equidistant from the Brahmaputra Valley and the plains of Central Burma, a natural halfway house and staging place for any great military movement in either direction between India and Burma.'[1]

—Field Marshal Viscount Slim, *Defeat into Victory*

IT WAS IN THE REGION that is sometimes referred to simply as the 'Northeast' that India felt the full force of the Second World War. For it was only here on the country's eastern frontier that the Allies and an Axis power—Japan—clashed on the ground. The fighting in 1944 was no minor affair: many now consider that the twin battles of Imphal and Kohima in Northeast India involved some of the

---

1 William J. Slim, *Defeat into Victory* (London: Cassell, 1956), pp. 330–31.

bitterest fighting seen anywhere during the war. Indeed, Imphal and Kohima together were arguably the defining moment of India's lived experience of the Second World War. But they were just part of a story that actually stretches for almost four years and one which saw the complete transformation of the region bordering Burma.

It should be made clear at the outset that for the purposes of this book and given its Second World War theme, by Northeast India one is referring to the present-day seven states of Arunachal Pradesh, Meghalaya, Mizoram, Nagaland, Assam, Manipur and Tripura. During the war, and before they were reconstituted in post-Independence India, the first four came under Assam, while Manipur and Tripura were separate princely states.

The Japanese take Burma[2]

Northeast India's experience from 1942 to 1945 has to be viewed in the context of the overall Burma Campaign. Considered the longest campaign on land fought by the British during the Second World War, it involved a struggle between the Allies and the Japanese for control of Burma. By virtue of its location on the India–Burma frontier, the Northeast was bound to be affected by the happenings next door. Until that time, however, all seemed by and large quiet in this region dominated by the valley of the Brahmaputra river and the mountainous, jungled terrain along the border with Burma.

Prior to 1942, in a sense the key book-end date which marks the beginning of the Northeast's tryst with the Second World War, few expected India to face danger from the east. If the war was to reach the country at all, it was expected from the usual direction used to invade India since time immemorial: from the north-west, via

---

2 Due to its resonance in all writings about the Second World War, this book uses the name Burma throughout.

Afghanistan. Consequently, little had been done by the British to prepare defences for an attack on India from the east. The defence of Burma and the British colonies in Southeast Asia was for all practical purposes entrusted to Singapore.

Then came the Japanese attack on Pearl Harbor in early December 1941 and the subsequent invasion of Allied colonies in Southeast Asia. The latter fell to the attackers like dominoes. What shocked the British the most was the fall of Singapore in mid-February 1942. Burma was to be next. Besides its ample natural resources, the country was from where the Allies were sending supplies over land via the Burma Road to Chiang Kai-shek and his Nationalist forces fighting the Japanese in China. The Chinese and the Japanese had been warring since 1937 and the latter had since occupied China's eastern seaboard. This meant that the Burma Road had become the main source of Allied supplies for China. Soon enough, the Japanese attacked, cut the Burma Road and captured Rangoon, Burma's capital. By May 1942, they had occupied most of Burma, arriving near the Chindwin river and at the doorstep of Northeast India.

Naturally, Northeast India felt the consequences of the fall of Burma. First came the refugees. As the Japanese captured more and more parts of Burmese territory in early 1942, they triggered an exodus of some 600,000 mainly Indian refugees (estimates vary). These were people who had settled in Burma under British rule and who had, over time, come to dominate the Burmese economy. They included professionals and civil servants, as well as dockyard workers, coolies and labourers. Increasing Burmese resentment of their presence had led to anti-Indian riots in the 1930s. As the British authorities fled in 1942, so did many Indians. They were fearful and uncertain not just about their new Japanese rulers, but of how they might be treated by the Burmese under their rule.

Once the sea route of escape out of the country was closed by the Japanese advance, hundreds of thousands of refugees headed north in a desperate scramble—towards Northeast India. For this was where the last remaining entry points into India lay. By one account, nearly 200,000 refugees entered India through Moreh in Manipur in the first half of 1942; some tens of thousands came in through the Pangsau Pass further north in what is Arunachal Pradesh today. Many thousands are said to have died in their escape out of Burma and over the treacherous mountainous terrain of the India–Burma frontier. The refugees passed through Imphal and towns in Assam in an attempt to reach beyond the Brahmaputra river. En route, they received whatever limited assistance the ill-prepared authorities in India could provide. This included, among others, support from the Maharaja of Manipur in Imphal, the British deputy commissioner in Kohima and the Indian Tea Association in Assam.

The refugees were not the only ones headed to Northeast India. In came also the British military force in Burma (Burma Corps) that had completed the longest retreat in British military history when it entered Moreh in Manipur in May 1942. Defeated and chased by the Japanese along the length of the country, the British had retreated some 1,500 km. The American General Joe Stilwell also reached Imphal, as did thousands of Chinese soldiers, who had been part of the forces sent by Chiang Kai-shek to Burma to assist in stemming the Japanese advance. The majority of that force had escaped back into China via northern Burma.

As the monsoon set in that year, India waited with bated breath to see whether the Japanese would continue their lightning advance westwards over land from Burma. There was certainly nothing by way of prepared defences to stop them from entering India had they decided to do so. In the event, they chose not to. Having already achieved their main objective of cutting the Burma Road, the Japanese turned their attention to consolidating their hold over Burma and their recently acquired territories in Southeast Asia.

The Japanese were also dissuaded by the natural barrier in the form of the mountainous, jungle terrain of the India–Burma frontier. Their reservations about the feasibility of any large military force traversing these mountains would come to be challenged only later, in 1943; subsequently, an invasion would be planned for 1944. But until then, they would generally stay east of the Chindwin river. And Northeast India would settle into its role as a frontline in the Second World War.

Mountains in Manipur along the India–Burma frontier. This is a view off the Tamu–Palel Road near Tengnoupal village. Photo by Hemant Singh Katoch.

Khurai Chingambam Mandap, Imphal. This temple was bombed from the air by the Japanese on 20 April 1943. Photo by Hemant Singh Katoch.

Northeast India transforms

The Americans and the British differed in their objectives for Burma. The primary American aim was to restore a supply line to Chiang Kai-shek in China after the loss of the Burma Road. Washington wanted to keep the Chinese in the war; their involvement helped to tie down large numbers of Japanese soldiers who might otherwise be redirected to the fight with the Americans in the Pacific. The Americans also hoped that eventually they might be in a position to use airfields on the Chinese mainland to bomb Japan itself. Thus, for them, any action in Burma was to be aimed at restarting supplies to Chiang Kai-shek's forces. Northern Burma, as a conduit towards China, was their main concern.

The British were not as bothered about Northern Burma. They were smarting from their humiliating defeats in the region and wanted to take the fight back to the Japanese more directly. London would ideally have preferred the recovery of Singapore, but tackling Burma first seemed relatively more realistic. Not that the latter was expected to be easy. There was much wariness and scepticism about the prospects of an overland invasion, a belief that was strengthened after a failed British offensive in the Arakan (present-day Rakhine State), a coastal belt in western Burma, in early 1943. But the shortage of landing crafts in the region ruled out the immediate retaking of Rangoon via the amphibious route, the favoured option. On their part, the Americans did not look too kindly upon what they saw as British intentions to restore their lost colonial territories and prestige. Washington's view of prioritizing the restoration of supplies to the Chinese—via Northern Burma—prevailed and this became the main Allied objective in Burma.

Where the American and British did agree was in recognizing how strategically important Northeast India was to their aims. This region would serve as the launch pad from where supplies would be sent again to the Chinese. This was from where an overland Japanese attack on India could most likely come and from where an offensive in the opposite direction could be directed. But before the strategic advantages of the Northeast could be exploited something would have to be done—and soon—about its dismal infrastructure. And so began, thanks to the Second World War, the most dramatic and rapid transformation of Northeast India's infrastructure in its history.

The construction of airfields became a priority for the Allies. The Americans wanted to resume supplying the Chinese and the quickest way to do so was to fly supplies over the Eastern Himalayas—nicknamed the 'Hump'—from Northeast India to Kunming in China's Yunnan province. This required the presence of multiple airfields located as far east as possible. Thus came up a number of runways carved out of the jungle or tea plantations in Assam, many clustered around the town of Dibrugarh. This included the airfield that later became Dibrugarh Airport—Mohanbari—as well as others such as Sookerating, Dinjan, Chabua, Ledo and Jorhat. Other airfields in Northeast India that came up during the Second World War included Tulihal (present-day Imphal Airport), Kumbhirgram (present-day Silchar Airport), Dimapur (present-day Dimapur Airport) and Agartala (present-day Agartala Airport).

Roads were also overhauled in support of the war effort. It was perhaps Manipur that saw the most activity in road construction and rehabilitation. As Imphal was developed into a forward supply base, roads across the then-princely state were upgraded. Dirt tracks were worked on and made 'jeepable', others were converted to tarmac, while some stretches had to be carved out afresh in the mountains. Ironically enough, many of these would be used by the Japanese Fifteenth Army in its offensive aimed at Imphal in 1944.

Farther north, the Americans began constructing what has since become famous as the Ledo or Stilwell Road. Originating from the town of Ledo in Assam, it was so named after 'Vinegar

Joe' Stilwell, the top US general in what the Americans called the China–Burma–India (CBI) theatre of the Second World War. The aim was for the Stilwell or Ledo Road to cut through the thick jungles of Northern Burma and link up to part of the old Burma Road into China. While the flights over the Hump had allowed the Americans to quickly resume sending supplies to the Chinese, it was with the Ledo Road that Stilwell intended to eventually replace the loss of the Burma Road.

Something also had to be done about the rickety railway that serviced Northeast India. Its tonnage of a few hundred tonnes per day may have been sufficient to meet the peacetime demands of tea plantations and coal mines, but it was wholly inadequate for the role the Bengal and Assam Railway was asked to play after the Japanese had taken over Burma. Over time, this included carrying supplies that would be flown to China from the airfields around Dibrugarh, transporting soldiers to Dimapur to be deployed to the forward areas, besides moving provisions and materials to maintain the Allied forces in Northeast India. Work was done to increase the monthly tonnage of the railway manifold during the war years.

The Second World War also brought with it for the first time to the Northeast large numbers of soldiers from other parts of India and the world. The threat posed by the Japanese next door had to be met by men on the ground to defend India's frontier with Burma. 4 Corps (of the Eastern Army at the time) was deployed to the region; in time, most of what became the British Fourteenth Army would pass through Northeast India. Supply and fuel depots and other support facilities came to dot the Imphal Valley, Dimapur, and other locations that saw a large military presence.

The jungles and mountains that made up most of the India–Burma frontier were too vast for the newly arrived soldiers to cover, however. They needed more eyes and ears to be on constant lookout for any Japanese activity in the area. One answer to the problem was V Force. This was essentially an intelligence-gathering force consisting of thousands of men from the hill tribes, under the command of a handful of British officers and other personnel. The most famous was the anthropologist Ursula Graham Bower, who commanded a force of Nagas in Assam's Cachar Hills. Members of V Force were to prove useful as the British went about strengthening their military presence in the forward areas.

A tree next to the old Ledo Airfield.
Photo by Findlay Kimber.

The Ledo/Stilwell Road seen through the forest cover as it makes its way towards Northern Burma.
Photo by Findlay Kember.

The first Chindit operation: Operation Longcloth

Along the India–Burma frontier through the rest of 1942 and early 1943, the main action had been the failed British offensive in the Arakan. Coming as it did not long after their evacuation from Burma, this added to the gloom among the Allies in the Burma theatre of war. What finally helped lift spirits was Operation Longcloth, or what is commonly referred to as the first Chindit operation. Launched in February 1943 from Imphal, this entailed the sending of some 3,000 men as part of long-range penetration groups deep inside Japanese-held territory in Burma. Their aim was to disrupt Japanese supply and communication lines in the targeted area, and they set off under the command of the British Brigadier Orde Wingate, who had conceptualized the operation.

Longcloth is said to have not had much of an impact militarily; of far greater importance was the publicity around this operation and its boost to Allied morale. On their part, the Japanese in Burma certainly took notice of Operation Longcloth. What they looked at closely was the fact that several thousand soldiers had been able to set off from Northeast India, cross the mountainous India–Burma frontier, and target their supply lines. It showed that a large military force could cross these seemingly impassable mountains. They also wondered if Operation Longcloth was a precursor to a larger Allied invasion of Central Burma. Such an invasion had to be pre-empted and planning began for a Japanese offensive in India.

It should be noted that the intention of the highest levels of the Japanese military leadership was that the operation be essentially defensive in nature—to better defend Burma. That is, it was aimed at preventing an Allied offensive down the same route. Its main objective was the capture of Imphal in Manipur, the reason being that the Imphal Valley was the only bit of flatland in an otherwise mountainous area. As Slim had noted, this provided the easiest route for any large military force to travel between India and Burma. Taking Imphal would effectively block any planned invasion of Central Burma.

Lieutenant General Mutaguchi Renya, whose Fifteenth Army was to carry out the operation, had much more ambitious ideas, however. With its large supply depots and the railway line carrying Allied supplies for the Chinese to Ledo, he privately felt that he could aim for Dimapur, and farther afield. Mutaguchi's views found the support of Subhas Chandra Bose, who in 1943 had taken over the reins of the Indian National Army (INA). The INA consisted of Indian prisoners of war captured by the Japanese in Malaya and Singapore after their defeat of the (British-led) Indian Army in 1942. Bose believed that once the INA had broken through into India, initially with Japanese help, it would be welcomed by ordinary Indians. It could then aim to 'march to Delhi' and start to realize the objective of its creation—to liberate India militarily from British rule.

Imperial General Headquarters in Tokyo issued a directive in early January 1944, giving the green light for an operation in India. The capture of Imphal was to be its primary objective, 'in order to defend Burma'.[3] And thus the stage was set for a great battle in Northeast India in 1944.

---

3 United States Army, *Burma Operations Record: 15th Army Operations in Imphal Area and Withdrawal to Northern Burma* (Japan, 1957), p. 78.

The world visits Northeast India

The Burma Campaign of the Second World War brought hundreds of thousands of people from around the country and the world to Northeast India for the first and last time. Never before had so many people from foreign lands come here; nor have they done so again since. The period of 1942–45 was, in a sense, the last time the world came to visit the Northeast.

There were the Americans who flew the Hump route to China, as well as those involved in the construction of the Ledo or Stilwell Road. Merrill's Marauders passed through en route to Northern Burma. Members of the American Field Service helped evacuate casualties from the front at Imphal. Canadians, Australians and New Zealanders also flew Allied planes, notably to assist in the defence of Imphal and Kohima in 1944.

Chinese soldiers were in the region. Many flew in over the Hump to the airfields around Dibrugarh and went on to central India for training. They returned to carry on to Northern Burma as part of X Force. The Japanese came attacking the Fifteenth Army in Manipur and the Naga Hills as part of the U-Go offensive.

Indians from Southeast Asian countries came to Manipur as part of the INA, facing off with Gurkhas from Nepal as well as other Indians from different parts of the country in the British Fourteenth Army. The latter fought alongside many fellow soldiers who would go on to become Pakistanis and Bangladeshis after 1947 and the creation of Bangladesh in 1971.

Perhaps most intriguingly, soldiers from several African territories ruled by the British came to Northeast India during the war. These included places that would later go on to become independent African countries, such as Kenya, Tanzania, Malawi and Uganda, among others. The African soldiers entered the Kabaw Valley in Burma via Imphal to go after the retreating Japanese following their defeat at Imphal and Kohima.

Some forty Africans lie buried today at the Imphal War Cemetery, thousands of miles away from home. Their graves, those of other Allied troops and personnel in this and the four other Commonwealth War Graves Commission (CWGC) cemeteries in the region, the Japanese memorials, the Chinese buried at Jairampur—all of them serve to remind us of a time when Northeast India found itself as a sudden and dramatic setting for the Second World War.

2

The Warring Sides

'Since the British lived on islands off the coast of Europe six thousand miles to the west and the Japanese on similar islands off the coast of Asia several thousand miles to the east, a clash in the remote area of the Indo-Burmese border may seem a strange confrontation.'[4]

—Ian Lyall Grant, *Burma: The Turning Point*

British Fourteenth Army

The Fourteenth Army had been created out of the former Eastern Army in August 1943. It came under the newly established South East Asia Command, of which Vice Admiral Lord Louis Mountbatten had been appointed Supreme Allied Commander. Lieutenant General William J. Slim was given the command of the Fourteenth Army. This was an enlightened choice as there was perhaps no other British

---

4 Ian Lyall Grant, *Burma: The Turning Point* (Barnsley: Leo Cooper, 2003), pp. 19–20.

commander who was better suited to lead in the crucial fight that lay ahead against the Japanese in Burma.

Slim certainly had ample experience with the Japanese in the field: he had been hastily summoned to take charge of Burma Corps in the retreat from Burma in 1942. Then, in 1943, he had again been sent to the rescue of a British force in the failed first operation against the Japanese in the Arakan. Importantly, Slim had learnt lessons from these defeats, and he sought to draw on them to ensure his army was better prepared in any future fight with the Japanese. He implemented a rigorous training regime for the men of the Fourteenth Army. Jungle warfare was a particular focus. He knew that in order to face the Japanese his men needed to become similarly adept and comfortable in operating in the jungle. Over time, this would lead his men to believe that they were more than a match for the Japanese and that there was little to fear about encountering them in a hitherto alien and intimidating jungle environment.

Slim also ensured that his men were well taken care of: robust arrangements were put in place to ensure they had improved medical and logistical support, and more secure supply and communication lines. Better air and ground coordination was put into effect; a key benefit of this would be that cut off or surrounded units would henceforth be kept supplied by air. All of these measures did wonders for the morale of the men. And so, by 1944, the Fourteenth Army was—compared to the defeated British force of 1942—far better trained, logistically supported, and more disciplined to face the Japanese in battle.

Slim had two corps under his command in early 1944. There was 15 Corps, which was in the Arakan in Burma, and 4 Corps, which was headquartered at Imphal in Manipur. Kohima also initially came under the operational command of Lieutenant General Geoffrey Scoones at 4 Corps. The corps had three divisions: the 17th Indian

Division, the 20th Indian Division and the 23rd Indian Division. The first two were deployed just across the frontier in Burma around Tiddim and Tamu respectively, while the latter was in reserve around Imphal. These would soon be joined by additional forces once the Japanese offensive got under way: two brigades of the 5th Indian Division and one of the 7th Indian Division would be flown from the Arakan to Imphal. The remaining three brigades of these divisions would be flown to Dimapur (for Kohima), while the British 2nd Division would also be diverted there. All of these Kohima-bound formations would come under 33 Corps, commanded by Lieutenant General Stopford, by April.

In early 1944, 4 Corps had been preparing to launch a limited offensive into Burma in support of the Americans in the north of the country. But by then there was sufficient intelligence to indicate that the Japanese were planning their own offensive into India. It was expected to be launched by mid-March. This was the moment that Slim had been waiting for. He had wanted to face the Japanese on ground favourable to him and where, unlike in 1942, it was they who would have long and tenuous supply and communication lines behind them. Moreover, he wanted the clash to be a decisive one and to happen before his army entered Burma.

The strategy devised for 4 Corps was as follows: as soon as the expected Japanese offensive would get under way, the two divisions deployed across the frontier would carry out a controlled withdrawal to and around the Imphal Valley (also referred to as the Imphal Plain in some war accounts and Manipur Valley elsewhere). There, around Imphal, the Fourteenth Army would make its stand against the incoming Japanese force, which would find itself strung out over the mountainous India–Burma frontier. The attack would first be held on all fronts around Imphal, before the British force would counterattack, beat and pursue the defeated Japanese back into Burma.

Around Imphal, the Japanese attack was expected to come from two principal directions: from the south-west up the Tiddim Road, where the 17th Indian Division was, and from the south-east up the main road into Burma, the Tamu–Palel Road, where the 20th Indian Division was. North of Imphal, at most a Japanese regiment (or brigade) was expected to arrive, aimed at cutting the vital supply line of the Imphal–Kohima–Dimapur Road. With its forces deployed accordingly, the units of the Fourteenth Army waited for the expected Japanese onslaught in March 1944.

Japanese Fifteenth Army

The Japanese in Burma came under the Burma Area Army commanded by Lieutenant General Kawabe Masakazu. Selected for the planned offensive into India was its Fifteenth Army commanded by Lieutenant General Mutaguchi Renya. Mutaguchi was an ambitious and pugnacious man. He was among those who had initially been against the idea of a Japanese offensive into India when it had been first mooted after the takeover of Burma. The Chindit operation in 1943 had helped change his mind; over time he became the biggest champion of the cause, aggressively lobbying for it.

Mutaguchi had a poor opinion of British military capabilities in Southeast Asia. This was perhaps not unjustified given the disasters that had befallen the British in Singapore, Malaya and Burma and in the first Arakan operation. Where Mutaguchi erred was in not taking into account the evolution of his foe into a much more formidable fighting force since. Thus, in 1944 he expected the Fourteenth Army to be unable to put up much of a resistance to his own Fifteenth Army at Imphal and Kohima.

He also personally harboured a more ambitious objective for the operation than that set by the Imperial Japanese Army leadership in Tokyo. As noted earlier, the latter saw the offensive as being pre-emptive in nature, to better defend the Japanese in Burma by blocking the main Allied invasion route into the country via Imphal. The capture of Imphal was, therefore, to be its main objective, with Kohima as a secondary aim, to prevent any help being sent up via the main road from the Brahmaputra Valley. But for Mutaguchi, there was the tantalizing possibility to consider what the capture of Imphal and Kohima might pave the way for—perhaps an even deeper offensive into India in coordination with the INA? Mutaguchi was not at all averse to exploring this opportunity at the right time.

Available to Mutaguchi were three Japanese infantry divisions under the Fifteenth Army: the 15th Division, the 31st Division and the 33rd Division. They numbered around 84,000 men in total. Before his offensive into Northeast India in March 1944, however, Mutaguchi launched a diversionary attack on Slim's force in the Arakan in February. He sought to draw in Fourteenth Army reserves and direct attention away from the much larger Operation 'U-Go' that would be aimed at Imphal and Kohima. In the event, the Arakan move was rebuffed, epitomized by the Japanese defeat in the Battle of the Admin Box where besieged Fourteenth Army units were kept supplied by air. Mutaguchi nevertheless pressed ahead with U-Go.

Around Imphal, he knew that the British would expect him to attack up the roads from Burma to the south: the Tiddim Road and the Tamu–Palel Road. And he did intend to send his powerful 33rd Division this way. But Mutaguchi also planned a major thrust from the north, directed both at Imphal and Kohima. A direction from which Slim and Scoones were expecting at most the equivalent of a British brigade to come, Mutaguchi would send through two entire divisions: the 15th Division towards Imphal and the 31st Division to Kohima. His strategy was a clever one and it would very nearly succeed. Had that happened, then the small force advancing alongside his men towards Imphal would have been called upon to play a much bigger role. This force was the INA.

Indian National Army

The INA's presence as part of U-Go was negligible compared to the Fifteenth Army. It consisted mainly of some 6,000 men of the INA's 1st Division who had been rushed from Burma to take part in the Imphal offensive. They were under the command of Colonel Mohammad Zaman Kiani. There were also several hundred men each in irregular groups attached to the participating Japanese divisions, whose tasks included intelligence gathering, propaganda and inducing defections from the Fourteenth Army.

Subhas Chandra Bose was keen on his men being at the vanguard of the Japanese advance into India. He had resisted suggestions to break down his main formation into smaller units; he wanted the INA to be seen as an organized force involved in the offensive. As mentioned earlier, this was in fact the moment the INA had long been waiting for: to endeavour to liberate India from British rule militarily. Of course, it was the Japanese Fifteenth Army that was to first break down the door to India at Imphal in 1944. This would, the INA hoped, pave the way for it to advance deeper into India, rousing the masses into a wider revolt against British rule. Imphal would thus be that first crucial step for the INA in its desired march all the way to Delhi.

ORDERS OF BATTLE: IMPHAL AND KOHIMA

Order of Battle: British[5]

Headquarters, South East Asia Command (SEAC) (Vice Admiral Lord Louis Mountbatten)

11th Army Group (General Sir George Giffard)

Fourteenth Army (Lieutenant General William Slim)

Imphal

4 Corps (Lieutenant General Geoffrey Scoones)

Armour

254th Indian Tank Brigade (Brigadier Reginald Scoones)
- 3rd Carabiniers (M3 Lee/Grants [Medium tanks])
- 7th Cavalry (Stuarts [Light tanks])
- C Squadron, 150th Regiment Royal Armoured Corps
- 401st Field Squadron, Indian Engineers
- 3/4th Bombay Grenadiers, less one company (motorized)

Artillery
- 8th Medium Regiment, Royal Artillery
- 67th Heavy Anti-Aircraft Regiment, Royal Artillery
- 28th Light Anti-Aircraft Regiment, Royal Artillery
- 78th Light Anti-Aircraft Regiment, Royal Artillery
- 15th Punjab Anti-Tank Regiment

---

5   The primary source of these orders of battle is S. Woodburn Kirby, *The War Against Japan*, vol. 3 (Uckfield: The Naval & Military Press, 1961).

- One battery, 2nd Survey Regiment

Infantry

- 9th Jat Machine-Gun Battalion
- 15/11th Sikh Regiment
- Chins Hills Battalion, Burma Army
- 3rd Assam Rifles
- 4th Assam Rifles
- 78th Indian Infantry Company
- Kalibahadur Regiment (Nepalese)
- One Company Gwalior Infantry, Indian State Forces

17th Indian Light Division (Major General D.T. 'Punch' Cowan)

Artillery

- 21st Indian Mountain Regiment
- 29th Indian Mountain Regiment
- 129th Light Field Regiment, Royal Artillery
- 82nd Light Anti-Aircraft/Anti-Tank Regiment, Royal Artillery

Divisional Infantry

- 1st West Yorkshire Regiment
- 7/10th Baluch Regiment
- 4/12th Frontier Force Regiment

Infantry

- 48th Indian Brigade (Brigadier Cameron/Brigadier Hedley)
  - 9th Border Regiment
  - 2/5th Royal Gurkha Rifles
  - 1/7th Gurkha Rifles

- 63rd Indian Brigade (Brigadier Burton)
  - 1/3rd Gurkha Rifles
  - 1/4th Gurkha Rifles
  - 1/10th Gurkha Rifles

20th Indian Division (Major General Douglas Gracey)

Artillery

- 9th Field Artillery Regiment, Royal Artillery
- 114th Jungle Field Regiment, Royal Artillery
- 23rd Indian Mountain Regiment
- 55th Light Anti-Aircraft/Anti-Tank Regiment, Royal Artillery

Divisional Infantry

- 4/3rd Madras Regiment

Infantry

- 32nd Indian Brigade (Brigadier Mackenzie)
  - 1st Northamptonshire Regiment
  - 9/14th Punjab Regiment
  - 3/8th Gurkha Rifles

- 80th Indian Brigade (Brigadier Greeves)
  - 1st Devonshire Regiment
  - 9/12th Frontier Force Regiment
  - 3/1st Gurkha Rifles

- 100th Indian Brigade (Brigadier James)
  - 2nd Border Regiment
  - 14/13th Frontier Force Rifles
  - 4/10th Gurkha Rifles

23rd Indian Division (Major General Ouvry Roberts)

Artillery

- 158th Jungle Field Regiment, Royal Artillery
- 3rd Indian Field Regiment
- 28th Indian Mountain Regiment
- 2nd Indian Light Anti-Aircraft/Anti-Tank Regiment

Infantry

- 1st Indian Brigade (Brigadier King)
  - 1st Seaforth Highlanders
  - 1/16th Punjab Regiment
  - 1st Patiala Regiment, Indian State Forces
- 37th Indian Brigade (Brigadier Collingridge/Brigadier Marindin)
  - 3/3rd Gurkha Rifles
  - 3/5th Royal Gurkha Rifles
  - 3/10th Gurkha Rifles
- 49th Indian Brigade (Brigadier Esse)
  - 4/5th Mahratta Light Infantry
  - 6/5th Mahratta Light Infantry
  - 5/6th Rajputana Rifles

50th Indian Parachute Brigade (Brigadier Hope-Thomson/Brigadier Woods)

Infantry

- 152nd Indian Parachute Battalion
- 153rd Gurkha Parachute Battalion
- 50th Indian Parachute Machine-Gun Company

5th Indian Division (Major General Harold Briggs/Major General Evans) (Flown to Imphal from Arakan [Burma] in March)

Artillery

- 4th Field Regiment, Royal Artillery
- 28th Jungle Field Regiment, Royal Artillery
- 56th Light Anti-Aircraft/Anti-Tank Regiment, Royal Artillery
- 24th Indian Mountain Regiment

Divisional Infantry

- 3/2nd Punjab Regiment

Infantry

- 9th Indian Brigade (Brigadier Salomons)
  - 2nd West Yorkshire Regiment
  - 3/9th Jat Regiment
  - 3/14th Punjab Regiment
- 123rd Indian Brigade (Brigadier Evans/Brigadier Denholm-Young)
  - 2nd Suffolk Regiment
  - 2/1st Punjab Regiment
  - 1/17th Dogra Regiment

7th Indian Division (Flown to Imphal from Arakan in May)

- 89th Indian Brigade (Brigadier Crowther)
  - 2nd King's Own Scottish Borderers
  - 4/8th Gurkha Rifles
  - 1/11th Sikh Regiment

Kohima

33 Corps (Lieutenant General Montagu Stopford)

Armour

- 11th Cavalry
- 45th Cavalry
- 149th Regiment, Royal Armoured Corps
- Detachment, 150th Regiment, Royal Armoured Corps

Artillery

- 1st Medium Regiment, Royal Artillery
- 50th Indian Light Anti-Aircraft/Anti-Tank Regiment
- 24th Indian Mountain Regiment

Infantry

- 1st Burma Regiment
- 1st Chamar Regiment
- 1st Assam Regiment
- The Shere Regiment (Nepalese)
- The Mahindra Dal Regiment (Nepalese)

202 Line of Communication Area (Major General Ranking)

5th Indian Division (Flown to Dimapur from Arakan in March)

- 161st Indian Brigade (Brigadier D.F.W. Warren)
  - 4th Queen's Royal West Kents
  - 1/1st Punjab
  - 4/7th Rajputs

British 2nd Division (Major General J.M.L. Grover)

Artillery

- 10th Assault Field Regiment, Royal Artillery
- 16th Assault Field Regiment, Royal Artillery
- 99th Assault Field Regiment, Royal Artillery
- 100th Light Anti-Aircraft/Anti-Tank Regiment, Royal Artillery

Divisional Infantry

- 2nd Reconnaissance Regiment
- 2nd Manchester Machine-Gun Battalion (less one company)
- 143rd Special Service Company

Infantry

- 4th Brigade (Brigadier W.H. Goschen/Brigadier J.A. Theobalds /Brigadier R.S. McNaught)
  - 1st Royal Scots
  - 2nd Royal Norfolk Regiment
  - 1/8th Lancashire Fusiliers
- 5th Brigade (Brigadier V.F.S. Hawkins/Brigadier M.M. Alston-Roberts-West)
  - 7th Worcestershire Regiment
  - 2nd Dorsetshire Regiment
  - 1st Queen's Own Cameron Highlanders
- 6th Brigade (Brigadier J.D. Shapland/Brigadier W.G. Smith)
  - 1st Royal Welch Fusiliers
  - 1st Royal Berkshire Regiment
  - 2nd Durham Light Infantry

7th Indian Division (Major General Frank Messervy) (Flown from Arakan)

Divisional Infantry

- 7/2nd Punjab Regiment

Artillery

- 136th Field Regiment, Royal Artillery
- 139th Field Regiment, Royal Artillery
- 24th Anti-Tank Regiment, Royal Artillery
- 25th Mountain Regiment, Indian Army

Infantry

- 33rd Indian Brigade (Brigadier Loftus Tottenham)
  - 1st Queen's Royal Regiment
  - 4/15th Punjab
  - 4/1st Gurkha Rifles
- 114th Indian Brigade (Brigadier Roberts)
  - 1st Somerset Light Infantry
  - 4/14th Punjab Regiment
  - 4/5th Royal Gurkha Rifles

23rd Long Range Penetration Brigade

- 60th Field Regiment, Royal Artillery
- 2nd Duke of Wellington's Regiment
- 4th Border Regiment
- 1st Essex Regiment

268th Indian Brigade (Brigadier Dyer)

- 2/4th Bombay Grenadiers
- 5/4th Bombay Grenadiers
- 17/7th Rajput Regiment

Eastern Air Command: Calcutta (Major General G.E. Stratemeyer USAAF)

3rd Tactical Air Force: Comilla (Air Vice Marshal John Baldwin)

- 221 Group Royal Air Force: Imphal (Air Commodore S.F. Vincent)
    - 5 Squadron (Hurricane IIC)
    - 11 Squadron (Hurricane IIC)
    - 20 Squadron (Hurricane IID)
    - 28 Squadron (Hurricane IIC)
    - 34 Squadron (Hurricane IIC)
    - 42 Squadron (Hurricane IIC)
    - 60 Squadron (Hurricane IIC)
    - 81 Squadron (Spitfire VIII)
    - 84 Squadron (Vengeance)
    - 110 Squadron (Vengeance)
    - 113 Squadron (Hurricane IIC)
    - 123 Squadron (Hurricane IIC)
    - 136 Squadron (Spitfire VIII)
    - 152 Squadron (Spitfire VIII)
    - 176 Squadron (Beaufighter VIF)
    - 607 Squadron (Spitfire VIII)
    - 615 Squadron (Spitfire VIII)
    - 1 Indian Air Force Squadron (Hurricane IIB/IIC)
    - 7 Indian Air Force Squadron (Vengeance)
    - 9 Indian Air Force Squadron (Hurricane IIC)

Troop Carrier Command: Comilla (Brigadier William Old USAAF)

- 31 Squadron (Dakota)

- 62 Squadron (Dakota)
- 99 Squadron (Wellington X)
- 117 Squadron (Dakota)
- 194 Squadron (Dakota)
- 215 Squadron (Dakota/Wellington)
- 216 Squadron (Dakota)

Order of Battle: Japanese

Southern Army (Field Marshal Count Terauchi)

Burma Area Army (Lieutenant General Kawabe Masakazu)

Fifteenth Army (Lieutenant General Mutaguchi Renya)

Imphal

15th Division (Lieutenant General Yamauchi)

Artillery

- 21st Field Artillery Regiment

Infantry

- 51st Infantry Regiment (Colonel Omoto)
  - I Battalion
  - III Battalion
- 60th Infantry Regiment (Colonel Matsumura)
  - II Battalion
  - III Battalion
- 67th Regiment
  - II Battalion
  - III Battalion

33rd Division (Lieutenant General Yanagida/Lieutenant General Tanaka)

Armour

- 14th Tank Regiment (Colonel Ueda)

Artillery

- 33rd Mountain Artillery Regiment
- 3rd Heavy Field Artillery Regiment
- 18th Heavy Field Artillery Regiment

Infantry

- Infantry Group (Major General Yamamoto)
- 213th Regiment (Colonel Miyawaki)
  - II Battalion
  - III Battalion
- 214th Regiment (Colonel Sakuma)
  - I Battalion
  - II Battalion
  - III Battalion
- 215th Regiment (Colonel Sasahara)
  - I Battalion
  - II Battalion
  - III Battalion

Reinforcements

- 151st Regiment (less one battalion) (Colonel Hashimoto)
- II/154th Battalion
- I/67th Battalion
- I/60th Battalion

- II/51st Battalion
- 4th Independent Engineer Regiment
- 33rd Engineer Regiment

Kohima

31st Division (Lieutenant General Sato)

Artillery

- 31st Mountain Artillery Regiment

Infantry

- Infantry Group (Major General Miyazaki)
- 58th Regiment (Colonel Fukunaga)
  - I Battalion
  - II Battalion
  - III Battalion
- 124th Regiment (Colonel Miyamoto)
  - I Battalion
  - II Battalion
  - III Battalion
- 138th Regiment (Colonel Torikai)
  - I Battalion
  - II Battalion
  - III Battalion

31st Engineer Regiment

Japanese Army Air Force

5th Air Division (Major General Tazoe)
- 4th Air Brigade

- 50th Air Regiment (Nakajima Ki 43 'Oscar')
- 8th Air Regiment (Kawasaki Ki 48 'Lily')

- 7th Air Brigade
  - 64th Air Regiment (Nakajima Ki 43 'Oscar')
  - 204th Air Regiment (Nakajima Ki 43 'Oscar')
  - 12th Air Regiment (Mitsubishi Ki 21 'Sally')
  - 81st Air Regiment

62nd Air Regiment (Nakajima Ki 49 'Helen')

Order of Battle: INA

1st Division (Colonel Mohammad Zaman Kiani)

- 1st (Subhas) Brigade (less one battalion) (Lieutenant Colonel Shah Nawaz Khan)
- 2nd (Gandhi) Brigade (Lieutenant Colonel Inayat Jan Kiani)
- 3rd (Azad) Brigade (Lieutenant Colonel Gulzara Singh)

INA groups attached to each Japanese division

3

Chronology of Events

8 March	Japanese Fifteenth Army begins the offensive. 33rd Division is first off the mark in the Tiddim area (south of Imphal).
14 March	33rd Division cuts the Tiddim Road behind 17th Indian Division.
	17th Indian Division starts withdrawing from Tiddim.
15 March	Units of 23rd Indian Division, rushed south from Imphal to assist withdrawal of 17th Indian Division, come up against first Japanese roadblocks on the Tiddim Road.
	Japanese 15th and 31st Divisions cross the Chindwin river en route to Imphal and Kohima respectively.
26 March	Japanese take Nippon Hill on Shenam Saddle (Tamu–Palel Road) for the first time.

18–27 March	Fly-in of 5th Indian Division from Arakan to Imphal (9th Indian Brigade, 123rd Indian Brigade) and Dimapur (161st Indian Brigade).
22–26 March	Battle at Shangshak (Sangshak). 50th Indian Parachute Brigade delays the Japanese advance towards Kohima and Imphal.
24 March	Major General Wingate dies in a plane crash after taking off from Imphal.
27 March	British 2nd Division, en route to Arakan, is instructed to change course and head to Dimapur.
27 March–2 April	Battles at Jessami and Kharasom. Men of the 1st Assam Regiment take a stand against the advancing Japanese 31st Division.
28 March	Units of 23rd Indian Division fighting south and 17th Indian Division battling north make contact on the Tiddim Road. Honda Raiding Unit arrives on the Imphal–Kohima Road at Kangpokpi.
29 March	The Imphal–Kohima Road is cut by this day.[6]
1 April	First units of British 2nd Division arrive in Dimapur.
3 April	161st Indian Brigade is told to withdraw from Kohima and head towards Dimapur.

---

[6] There are multiple, differing accounts for when the bridge was blown. One puts it at late in the night of 28th March, while another has it on the 29th. Either way, by the latter date this vital road had been cut.

4 April	15th Division attacks features north and north-east of Imphal.
	Japanese 31st Division starts arriving in Kohima.
	17th Indian Division arrives in the Imphal Valley up the Tiddim Road.
	20th Indian Division completes withdrawal from Moreh on the Tamu–Palel Road.
5 April	Battalion of Royal West Kents (161st Indian Brigade) is rushed back up to Kohima.
6 April	Action at Runaway Hill north-east of Imphal, for which Abdul Hafiz wins posthumous Victoria Cross.
	Japanese force evacuation of Jail Hill at Kohima.
7 April	Lion Box at Kanglatongbi on the Imphal–Kohima Road is evacuated.
	Japanese 51st Regiment attacks Nungshigum, north-east of Imphal.
9 April	Action on Kohima Ridge, for which John Harman wins posthumous VC.
10 April	British abandon DIS Hill on Kohima Ridge to Japanese 31st Division.
	17th Indian Division is ordered to take over defence of the Tiddim Road and Silchar Track; 32nd Indian Brigade (20th Indian Division) comes under its command.
13 April	Japanese attack Sekmai, the closest they come to Imphal on the Imphal–Kohima Road.

	32nd Indian Brigade takes Point 5846 off the Silchar–Bishenpur Track.
	Japanese evicted from Nungshigum.
15 April	Japanese blow up the bridge on the Silchar–Bishenpur Track, cut the last road out of Imphal.
	23rd Indian Division takes over from 5th Indian Division on the Ukhrul Road.
16 April	Units of British 2nd Division moving up from Dimapur join with 161st Indian Brigade at Jotsoma.
	Yamamoto Force recaptures Nippon Hill on Shenam Saddle for the final time.
17 April	FSD Hill and Kuki Piquet on Kohima Ridge fall to the Japanese.
18 April	First troops from Jotsoma reach beleaguered British garrison at Kohima.
19 April	Japanese 15th Division abandons efforts to take Sekmai on the Imphal–Kohima Road and turns on the defensive north of Imphal.
20 April	Kohima Garrison is relieved by British 2nd Division.
22 April	Yamamoto Force captures Crete East and Cyprus on Shenam Saddle.
23 April	Japanese 31st Division fails to capture Garrison Hill on Kohima Ridge and turns on the defensive.
2 May	INA's attempted attack on Palel Airfield.

	9th Indian Brigade launches first attack on Hump on the Mapao–Molvom Range north of Imphal.
6 May	Action on GPT Ridge at Kohima, for which John Randle wins posthumous VC.
11 May	Yamamoto Force occupies part of Scraggy on Shenam Saddle.
13 May	All of Kohima Ridge is recovered from Japanese 31st Division.
13–16 May	20th Indian Division and 23rd Indian Division switch places on the Ukhrul Road and the Tamu–Palel Road.
17–24 May	Battle for Torbung Roadblock on the Tiddim Road.
20–26 May	Japanese attacks on Bishenpur on the Tiddim Road.
20–29 May	Battle for Point 2926/Red Hill on the Tiddim Road.
23 May	7th Indian Division is given responsibility for Naga (Kohima) village area. British 2nd Division concentrates on evicting Japanese from Aradura Spur area.
24 May	Yamamoto Force captures Gibraltar, the farthest limit of their advance on the Shenam Saddle (Tamu–Palel Road). It is evicted the same day.
31 May	Lieutenant General Sato orders 31st Division to withdraw from Kohima.

3 June	5th Indian Division ordered to intensify offensive up the Imphal–Kohima Road.
	Japanese 31st Division begins withdrawal from the Aradura Spur area at Kohima.
7 June	Action at Ningthoukhong, for which Hanson Victor Turner wins posthumous VC.
12 June	Last major Japanese attack on Ningthoukhong. Ganju Lama wins VC.
21–26 June	Japanese 151st Regiment launches attacks on piquets off the Silchar–Bishenpur Track.
22 June	British 2nd Division moving south and 5th Indian Division fighting north meet near Milestone 109 on the Imphal–Kohima Road and end the siege of Imphal.
26 June	Actions at Mortar Bluff and Water Piquet off the Silchar–Bishenpur Track, for which Netrabahadur Thapa and Agan Singh Rai win VCs.
8 July	Ukhrul falls to 33 Corps.
16 July	17th Indian Division clears last Japanese resistance at Ningthoukhong Kha Khunou on Tiddim Road.
	Japanese withdrawal from around Imphal begins.
24 July	Final assault to evict Japanese from Shenam Saddle, their last stronghold around Imphal.

4

Battle Sites

'The story of the prolonged and hard-fought battle of Imphal–Kohima that developed from the plans of Japanese and British commanders is not easy to follow. It swayed back and forth through great stretches of wild country; one day its focus was a hill named on no map, the next a miserable unpronounceable village a hundred miles away. Columns, brigades, divisions, marched and counter-marched, met in bloody clashes, and reeled apart, weaving a confused pattern hard to unravel.'[7]

—Field Marshal Viscount Slim, *Defeat into Victory*

The twin battles of Imphal and Kohima

The primary objective of the Japanese Fifteenth Army when it attacked India in March 1944 was the capture of Imphal, and two of its three divisions headed towards Manipur's capital. A third sought

---

7   Slim, *Defeat into Victory*, p. 341.

to cut the Dimapur–Kohima–Imphal Road, the main supply route into Imphal, as it crosses the mountains at Kohima. Thus the fighting at Imphal and Kohima were part of one large clash between the Fourteenth Army and the Fifteenth Army. The way the battles at the two places unfolded, however, make them seem almost independent of each other.

The Kohima battle lasted from early April to early June 1944 and involved two phases. The first was the famous siege of Kohima for a fortnight in April in which some 1,500 soldiers defended positions on the Kohima Ridge against a Japanese force of 15,000 men. The latter belonged to its 31st Division, who nearly succeeded in capturing the ridge. The siege ended with the arrival of reinforcements, mainly in the form of the British 2nd Division, as well as units from the 7th Indian Division. And so began the second phase of the Kohima battle—the gruelling task of evicting the Japanese from the Ridge and the surrounding heights of Kohima. This lasted until early June when the Japanese at long last withdrew from the Kohima area.

To the south, the Japanese laid siege to the Imphal Valley. Men of the 15th and 33rd Divisions had cut all of the routes leading to Imphal by April. From then until the end of June the Japanese struggled unsuccessfully to advance on Imphal from multiple directions. On and around each of the routes, the Japanese advance was met, held and eventually pushed back following intense fighting. The encircled British, Indian and Gurkha units were kept supplied by air and could rely on the six airfields that dotted the Imphal Valley. With the opening of the Imphal–Kohima Road on 22 June 1944 by the 5th Indian Division fighting northwards from Imphal and the

British 2nd Division advancing south from Kohima, the Japanese offensive was defeated. They would, however, continue to put up a fight around Manipur through the month of July.

Imphal and Kohima together are considered among Japan's largest-ever defeats on land. Some 30,000 Japanese are believed to have died and 23,000 injured in the fighting, due to disease, and in the retreat back to Burma. For the British forces, the corresponding figure is 16,000 dead and injured, with Imphal accounting for the overwhelming majority of casualties on both sides. Seven Victoria Crosses, the highest British military decoration for bravery, were awarded—five for actions around Imphal and two at Kohima.

The action on the ground at Imphal and Kohima in 1944 was complemented by furious activity in the air. Some 30,000 Allied sorties are estimated to have been flown during the battles in Manipur and the Naga Hills of Assam; the corresponding figure for the Japanese is some 1,750 sorties. The aircraft carried supplies, brought reinforcements, evacuated casualties, supported infantry operations, and bombed Japanese supply lines in Burma. Hundreds of Allied and Japanese planes flew in the skies of Northeast India in an aviation spectacle the likes of which the region—and India—had never seen before.

The outcome at Imphal and Kohima set the clock ticking on Japanese control of Burma. It weakened the overall Burma Area Army which was then unable to defend itself against the Fourteenth Army's subsequent invasion of Central Burma. In less than a year after Imphal and Kohima, the Allies had taken Rangoon (Yangon).

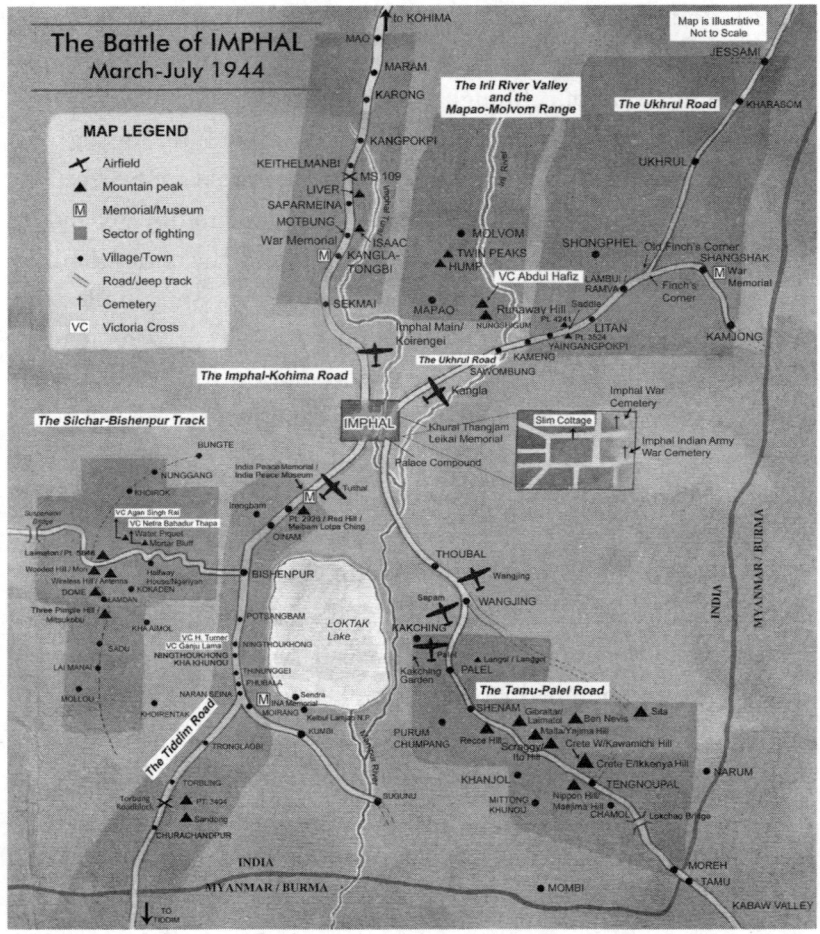

The Battle of Imphal

Courtesy of Robin Wahengbam, Hemant Singh Katoch and Hemam Bishwajeet Singh.

Imphal

'I imagine that every teenager today has heard of Stalingrad and Alamein and D-Day, but I wonder how many know the name of Imphal, that "Flower on Lofty Heights" where Japan suffered the greatest catastrophe in its military history.'[8]

—George MacDonald Fraser, *Quartered Safe Out Here*

Battle narrative

Imphal was the main prize the Japanese sought as they invaded India in 1944. Based on their past experience of fighting British forces, the operation was predicted to be swift. Mutaguchi certainly expected to wrap things up in some three weeks or so, and well before the Japanese Emperor's birthday on April 29. It was not to be, with deadly consequences for the Japanese.

Travelling light, with tenuous supply lines behind them, the ample provisions of the Imphal-based 4 Corps were supposed to fall easily to Mutaguchi's army. But they did not; neither did the British, Indian and Gurkha units panic and try to escape, despite the Japanese cutting all of the roads leading to Imphal. Instead, the men of the Fourteenth Army stood their ground and fought back. Most importantly, they were kept supplied and received reinforcements by air; the airfields in the Imphal Valley proving decisive to their sustenance and eventual victory.

With their tight timetable having gone awry, Japanese woes were compounded once the monsoon rains began in full earnest in May, making the difficult terrain ever more treacherous. The result was

---

8 George MacDonald Fraser, *Quartered Safe Out Here: A Harrowing Tale of World War II* (New York: Akadine Press, 2001), p. 3.

mass casualties for the Fifteenth Army—in combat as well as due to disease, and in the eventual retreat to Burma.

Imphal is a confusing battle to follow. Perhaps the best way to grasp it is to refer to the 'hub and spoke' analogy Slim used to describe Imphal in his book *Defeat into Victory*. He wrote that one way to understand how the diffuse fighting across Manipur and the India–Burma frontier unfolded is by thinking of Imphal as the 'hub' of a wheel, with the main routes heading to the town as its 'spokes':

Slim identified the spokes as follows:
- The Tiddim Road
- The Silchar–Bishenpur Track
- The Tamu–Palel Road
- The Ukhrul Road
- The footpath down the Iril River Valley
- The Kohima Road

The Japanese approached Imphal via these very spokes for the most part and it was on and around them that the bulk of the fighting took place in 1944.

Battlefield guide

Today, there is much to see in Manipur related to the Second World War, as the former princely state was arguably the most affected in the Northeast—nay, India—by the events of 1942–45. Besides the cemeteries, memorials and museums, what is truly special in Manipur are its battlefields dating back to 1944. For here is an entire collection of different landscapes connected to the war: from isolated peaks to a collection of hills, from a village stream to an old airfield. Some have changed over time, while others remain untouched, and include remains of bunkers and trenches. It is the discovery of these sites in the environs of Imphal that places Manipur as the foremost Second World War battlefield tourism destination of India.

The battlefields of Imphal are spread out across the state of Manipur. This should come as no surprise: the battle in 1944 involved the Japanese approaching Imphal from many directions and on all of them they were first halted and subsequently pushed back. Pitched battles were, therefore, fought on and around all of the main approach routes to Imphal. What is then the best way for someone to plan and structure a visit to the main battlefields in Manipur today? Slim's 'hub and spoke' analogy offers a useful guide. This book draws on it and suggests taking a sector-wise approach along the lines of the broad directions and 'spokes' from which the Japanese had approached Imphal. These would be:

- The Tiddim Road and the Silchar–Bishenpur Track (the south-west)
- The Tamu–Palel Road and the Shenam Saddle (the south-east)
- The Ukhrul Road and the Iril River Valley (the north-east)
- The Mapao–Molvom Range and the Imphal–Kohima Road (the north)

Let us consider each of these areas, both in terms of the events of 1944, and the battlefields and other sites of relevance to the Second World War that can be accessed today. A good place to begin would be the present-day city of Imphal, the primary objective of the Japanese U-Go offensive and the main starting point for most visitors to Manipur.

Imphal War Cemetery.
Photo by Hemant Singh Katoch.

Slim Cottage in the Kangla Fort Complex, Imphal.
Photo by Hemant Singh Katoch.

1. Imphal

In a sense, the clash in 1944 was a battle *for* Imphal rather than *of* Imphal. The Japanese were prevented from capturing Imphal and all the fighting at the time involved their efforts to try and reach the town. Imphal emerged largely untouched in 1944, all the fighting having raged around it. It thus does not have any erstwhile battlefields to visit; rather it has several sites related to its broader experience of the war.

- Cemeteries

The most prominent of such sites are the cemeteries: Imphal is the only city in India to house two cemeteries dedicated to the Second World War. Set up and maintained by the Commonwealth War Graves Commission (CWGC), these immaculate cemeteries are home to the graves of Commonwealth soldiers who fought in and around Manipur and the surrounding region during the war. Some 1,600 soldiers from a number of countries such as the UK, Canada, Australia, New Zealand, Kenya, Tanzania and elsewhere lie buried in the Imphal War Cemetery in the neighbourhood of Dewlahland.

A second, smaller CWGC cemetery is the Imphal Indian Army War Cemetery in the neighbourhood of Hatta. Here lie buried 828 Muslim soldiers from the (British-era) Indian Army. The cemetery also contains a cremation memorial, which commemorates 868 Hindu and Sikh soldiers killed during the Second World War.

- Slim Cottage, Kangla Fort

Another place of interest is the so-named Slim Cottage in the Kangla Fort in the heart of Imphal. The fort complex itself is a must-visit site, considering Kangla was for long the seat of Manipur's kings and the entire area today is an oasis of calm and greenery in an increasingly frenetic city. The cottage is a colonial-era building where Lieutenant General Slim had stayed for several months in 1944. This was after the battles at Imphal and Kohima, as the Fourteenth Army headquarters moved eastwards towards Burma. While the cottage can usually be viewed only from the outside, if one is lucky one can sometimes get the opportunity to explore its interiors.

- Khurai Chingangbam Mandap

A local memorial to the war can be found in the neighbourhood of Khurai in Imphal. There is a temple there—the Khurai Chingangbam Mandap—which was bombed from the air by the Japanese on 20 April 1943. The aerial bombing happened during a traditional feast and some ninety people are estimated to have died as a result. This is considered the largest loss of civilian lives in a single incident in Manipur during the Second World War. Today a small memorial in the temple premises commemorates the event. There is also a painting by a local artist, which is a reproduction of an old photo showing British officials inspecting the temple in the wake of the bombing in 1943.

- RKCS Art Gallery

Several more paintings depicting scenes of the war and the experience of the local population can be seen at the RKCS Art Gallery in Imphal.

- Imphal War Museum

In 2014 the city saw the opening of the private Imphal War Museum. Set up within the residence of a local war enthusiast, this contains the personal collections of war relics and artefacts that have been painstakingly gathered over the years from around Manipur.

- Imphal Main Airfield

Finally, there is an abandoned war-era airfield on the northern outskirts of Imphal at Koirengei. This was known as Imphal Main during the war and it was in its vicinity that 4 Corps headquarters was set up. This is covered in the later section about the Imphal–Kohima Road.

Cremation Memorial, Imphal Indian Army War Cemetery.
Photo by Hemant Singh Katoch.

Exhibits from the Imphal War Museum, a local
war-enthusiast-driven initiative.
Photo by Findlay Kember.

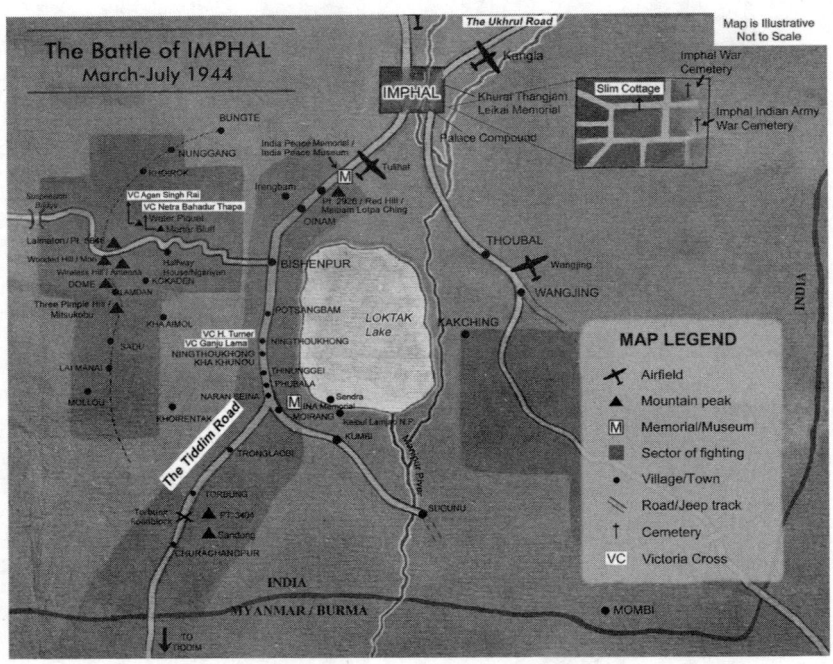

The Tiddim Road and the Silchar–Bishenpur Track
Courtesy of Robin Wahengbam, Hemant Singh Katoch and Hemam Bishwajeet Singh.

2. The Tiddim Road and the Silchar–Bishenpur Track

'It was along the Tiddim Road and the Silchar–Bishenpur track, the southern and western spokes of the wheel, that some of the heaviest fighting of this Battle of Attrition took place.'[9]

—Field Marshal Viscount Slim, *Defeat into Victory*

Battle narrative

It was the Japanese 33rd Division under the command of Lieutenant General Yanagida that approached Imphal from the south. Its men were sometimes also referred to as the White Tigers, a nod to an old Japanese legend of the area back home from which one of its regiments came. Considered a powerful formation, this division advanced on Imphal via the two southern routes from Burma: the Tiddim Road in the south-west and the Tamu–Palel Road in the south-east. This section deals with the former.

The Tiddim Road was the route that connected Imphal to Tiddim in the Chin Hills of Burma, a distance of some 264 km. The India section of the road was some 116 km, while the rest was in Burma. Except for the stretch in the flat Imphal Valley, for most of its length this fair-weather road twisted and turned through the hills of Manipur and the Chin Hills. For the Fourteenth Army in early 1944, this road was supporting the deployment and operations of the 17th Indian Division, commanded by Major General 'Punch' Cowan, in and around Tiddim. Men of this division were sometimes known as the Black Cats because of the divisional emblem of a black cat. The division was to withdraw up the road once the Japanese offensive got under way; it would then make its stand in the Imphal Valley.

---

9   Slim, *Defeat into Victory*, p. 377.

On his part, Mutaguchi instructed Yanagida to set off on 8 March, a week before the 15th and 31st Divisions further north were to advance. The idea was that the White Tigers would move swiftly to, first, cut off the route of withdrawal of the Black Cats, and second, destroy them, before heading to Imphal. The plight of the Indian division was also expected to draw in more reserves from 4 Corps, leaving a relatively ill-defended Imphal ripe for the taking.

The fighting on the Tiddim Road from March to July 1944 involved this clash between the Black Cats and the White Tigers. The initial stage in March entailed the Japanese cutting the road behind the 17th Indian Division—and the latter's subsequent successful push to fight its way through. In this it was helped by units of the 23rd Indian Division who had been rushed south from Imphal. This took place on the Burma side of the Tiddim Road, which is beyond the purview of this battlefield guide.

The Black Cats and those who assisted them withdrew to the Imphal Valley in early April. In the process, the Japanese 33rd Division had been given a bloody nose: they had suffered a couple of thousand casualties and been weakened even before they came close to Imphal. From then on the fighting consisted of Japanese attempts to get past the 17th Indian Division's defences and the latter's foiling of this effort, before going on the counteroffensive.

Closely connected to events on the Tiddim Road in the valley were the clashes in the hill range to the west. In fact, once they arrived in the valley, the bulk of the Japanese force in this sector took to these hills in their advance on Imphal; another column moved in parallel on the road itself. In the hills, it was in the vicinity of the Silchar–Bishenpur Track (or the Silchar Track) where much of the fighting took place. This track originated from Bishenpur on the Tiddim Road. Snaking its way westwards over the hills, it wriggled all the way through to Silchar in Assam. The stretch of the track from

Bishenpur to the top of the western hill range was the scene of the most action in 1944.

In terms of more specific phases of the fighting, in April 1944 the Japanese had come up against the British defences in this southwestern sector. May was the crucial month, which saw a clash between the main strategies of the White Tigers and the Black Cats, with Bishenpur, which was then a village, at the heart of it all. The Japanese sought to launch a multi-pronged attack on the main British defensive position in and around the village, while the 17th Indian Division attempted a hammer-and-anvil strategy to try and crush the Japanese. The month of June saw the Japanese launch their last serious—but ultimately unsuccessful—attacks. By July the scales had well and truly tilted in favour of the Fourteenth Army; by the middle of that month, the last of the major Japanese positions on the road in the Imphal Valley had been cleared.

Except at the start of the offensive, it was from this direction that the Japanese posed the greatest threat to Imphal through those crucial months of 1944. Mutaguchi himself moved to the western hill range alongside the Tiddim Road for over a fortnight in May and early June to more closely direct operations. This sector is also where some of the most intense fighting of the entire Imphal battle took place. Indeed, of the five Victoria Crosses won at Imphal, two each were awarded for actions on the Tiddim Road and just off the Silchar Track. Through it all, and despite their evident failure to break through to Imphal, the Japanese simply refused to give up, although the same could be said of their behaviour all around Imphal and Kohima.

Slim was to write later: 'There can have been few examples in history of a force as reduced, battered and exhausted as the 33rd Japanese Division delivering such furious assaults, not with the object of extricating itself, but to achieve its original offensive intention.'[10]

---

10 Slim, *Defeat into Victory*, p. 386.

He continued, 'Whatever one may think of the military wisdom of thus pursuing a hopeless object, there can be no question of the supreme courage and hardihood of the Japanese soldiers who made the attempts. I know of no army that could have equalled them.'[11]

Battlefield guide

This tour takes in the main sites of interest on and around the stretch of the Tiddim Road in the Imphal Valley. If a visitor to Manipur has only one full day to spare to explore the Second World War battlefields around Imphal, then this is probably the best sector to cover. Included en route are battlefields, memorials, two war museums and the stunning Loktak Lake.

- Tulihal Airfield (Bir Tikendrajit International Airport)

As you head out on the Tiddim Road, you pass Imphal's airport on your left on the outskirts of the town. This airport owes its existence to the Second World War. Then known as the Tulihal Airfield, this was one of six airfields that had come up in Manipur during the war. Besides playing a role in the Imphal battle, this airfield was also among those used for the fly-in to Burma of the second Chindit expedition, Operation Thursday, in March 1944.

One story goes that Tulihal was supposed to be much shorter than the actual airfield that was constructed. This has been put down to a communication error between the Americans and the British. The former had wanted it to be some 'four thousand long', with feet being the implied unit of measurement. But off went the British engineers and built one in yards—a lot longer than originally planned. Thanks to this quirk of history, the longer-than-intended airfield continues to serve Manipur well as its sole airport today.

---

11 Ibid.

Red Hill or Point 2926 alongside the Tiddim Road.
Photo by Findlay Kember.

- Point 2926 (Red Hill)

The scenery starts to open up just after the airport, and villages, paddy fields and the western hills running alongside start to come into view. After crossing the village of Nambol, which was known as Buri Bazar at the time of the war, a solitary hill looms to the left, just off the Tiddim Road. This was what was known as Point 2926 or Red Hill, or Maibam Lotpaching locally. It is the battlefield closest to Imphal to the south.

This feature and the adjacent village of Maibam were the sites of a fierce battle towards the end of May 1944. On the night of 20–21 May, it was attacked by a force of some 500 Japanese soldiers who had descended from the hills and then advanced up the road. This was the northern prong of the 33rd Division's main attack on Bishenpur at this time; it was intended to prevent any reinforcements from Imphal from coming through on the Tiddim Road. But the Japanese had not realized that Point 2926 was important for another reason: it practically overlooked the 17th Indian Division headquarters that had recently been set up nearby. For Major General 'Punch' Cowan, the divisional commander, the arrival of so many Japanese so close to his headquarters was an especially unwelcome surprise. They had to be evicted, and soon. What followed was a fight for control of this hill and Maibam village.

The Japanese had been unable to overcome the platoon of the 7/10th Baluch Regiment that held the peak, Point 2926, when they first attacked. The former were soon concentrated in the southern part of the feature, including two positions called First Pimple and Second Pimple, and in the village. Unsurprisingly, the British force found it difficult initially to force out the Japanese. Three attempts were made, involving the infantry and armour, but with limited success. Although some ground was gained, the Japanese were immovable.

The task was finally given to 'Woodforce', formed around the headquarters of the 50th Indian Parachute Brigade and consisting of a composite force of infantry, armour, artillery and sappers. After heavy fighting, Woodforce finally recovered Red Hill and Maibam by 29 May. Hundreds of Japanese are said to have died in the process.

One cannot now tell that the area was the scene of such violence during the Second World War. Red Hill and Maibam lie quiet today, the former's heights distinguishable from miles around by the mobile phone towers that dot it. The northern parts of the feature are covered in trees, while the southern bits are barer. The clue to the area's past lies in the fact that there are two Japanese war memorials at the base of the hill and now a new museum.

- India Peace Memorial

The more conspicuous of the memorials is what is known as the India Peace Memorial. This was built by the Japanese government in 1994 to mark the 50th anniversary of the Imphal battle. It is a minimalist, stark-looking memorial, with its concrete walls and red sandstone flooring. At its northern end are three blocks of uncut red sandstone. One local theory goes that these denote drops of blood of Japanese, British and Indian soldiers who participated in the Imphal battle.

There is an inscription on the walls, both in English and Japanese, which reads as follows:

'This monument shall stand as a prayer for peace and a symbol of friendship between the peoples of Japan and India in memory of all those who lost their lives in India during the last world war.'

Standing in the memorial's compound, you get a good feel of Red Hill as a battlefield, as it towers dramatically on one side. On the other is the—often noisy—Tiddim Road, the route the Japanese had sought so desperately to advance on to Imphal in 1944.

India Peace Memorial. Photo by Yaiphaba Meetei Kangjam.

Japanese War Memorial, Maibam village. Photo by Findlay Kember.

- Japanese War Memorial

Right next to the India Peace Memorial is a smaller Japanese war memorial, albeit one which is arguably more atmospheric. This structure, with a more traditional design, pre-dates the official memorial by a couple of decades. Its construction was funded by former comrades of those Japanese soldiers who died in the battle here in May 1944 and it has several moving inscriptions in Japanese in tribute to the fallen.

As you explore the site, it is worth bearing in mind that, together with the India Peace Memorial nearby, this is the only such complex of Japanese war memorials to be found in India. In addition, in Irengbam further down the road and to the west, there is another small Japanese memorial to those who lost their lives in that village. This is not always easy to find or access, however, given that it lies tucked away in a private residential compound.

- Imphal Peace Museum

On 22 June 2019, as part of the 75th anniversary commemoration of the Imphal battle, a new Japanese-funded museum was inaugurated at the foot of Red Hill. A joint project of the Nippon Foundation and the Sasakawa Peace Foundation, in collaboration with the Government of Manipur, the Manipur Tourism Forum and the 2nd World War Imphal Campaign Foundation, the new Imphal Peace Museum is a welcome addition to ongoing efforts to preserve the memory and experience of the Second World War in Manipur. It not only showcases information and artefacts related to the battle, but looks at the post-war period as well.

The Imphal Peace Museum.
Photo by Hemant Singh Katoch.

- Bishenpur (Bishnupur)

Continuing on, the distance between the Tiddim Road and the western hill range starts to become ever narrower. Soon, up ahead it appears as if one of the spurs is touching the road itself. You are approaching Bishenpur (or Bishnupur locally), the village which was the main British defensive position in this sector. It is easy to see why the Bishenpur area was chosen by the 17th Indian Division: there were natural barriers on both sides of the road in the vicinity of the village. To the immediate west lay the hills and towards the east–north-east were the upper reaches of Loktak Lake. As veteran

British officers of the time later wrote: 'This was the sole place capable of prolonged defence on the southern approach to Imphal.'[12]

Today, Bishenpur is a busy little town through which the Tiddim Road passes. During the Imphal battle, Bishenpur was at the heart of the clash between the White Tigers and the Black Cats—to the extent that some veterans have described the battles in this sector as the battles of Bishenpur. The village and its environs were the primary obstacle in the White Tigers' planned march to Imphal; consequently, the Black Cats had to hold on to it at all costs. Bishenpur was also the starting point for the track to Silchar to the west. Adding to its importance was the 'Gun Box' position on its outskirts, which was where the artillery support of the 32nd Indian Brigade had been concentrated. The brigade was made primarily responsible for operations on and around the Silchar Track and from Gun Box it had ceaselessly fired 25-pounders, 3.7 inch howitzers, 6-pounders and anti-aircraft guns.

May 1944 was when the fighting in this sector most directly affected Bishenpur. In the first half of that month, the village was attacked on some four occasions by the Japanese Army Air Force in one of their rare such appearances during the battle. In the last ten days of May, the Japanese 33rd Division sent in two infantry attacks from the hills, with the junction of the Tiddim Road and the Silchar Track as the main target. These infantry assaults were part of the same northern prong that had included the attack on Red Hill. It was to be part of a coordinated attack on Bishenpur from the north, south and west. In the end, only this line of attack on Bishenpur went in. On both occasions, the Japanese were furiously counterattacked, including with tanks, and were wiped out. According to one

---

12 Antony Brett-James and Geoffrey Evans, *Imphal, A Flower on Lofty Heights* (London: Macmillan, 1962), p. 251.

estimate, some 360 of the 380 Japanese soldiers involved were lost at Bishenpur.

The Tiddim Road on the way to Bishenpur, with the western hills in the distance. Photo by Moirangthem Ranjit.

The banks of the small stream or *turel* that bisects the village of Potsangbam. This is a view of the stream east of the road. Photo by Findlay Kember.

- Potsangbam

Further on down the road is Potsangbam. Sometimes called 'Pots and Pans' by British soldiers at the time, this was the northernmost village on the Tiddim Road to come under prolonged Japanese control in 1944. Men of the Japanese column that was advancing up the road towards Bishenpur and Imphal had infiltrated into Potsangbam in April. There they dug in. A foray was attempted north-east of

Potsangbam in early May, but this was rebuffed. Days of fighting followed as the units under the 17th Indian Division's command at Bishenpur sought to clear the Japanese from the village.

The layout and vegetation of Potsangbam greatly hindered the Black Cats' efforts. Houses in the village—and indeed the entire settlement itself—were ringed by bamboo clumps, fruit trees and other foliage. Almost all of the houses had ponds in their compounds, and there were bunds and embankments everywhere. The village, much like most of the villages in the Imphal Valley, was surrounded by open paddy fields, which made it easy to spot anyone approaching from the outside. These factors played to the advantage of the Japanese, who were anyway past masters at stubborn defence. They were firmly ensconced.

The Fourteenth Army units thus found the going hard as they launched attack after attack on the Japanese in the village. Every tactic was tried. This included pattern bombing Potsangbam and Ningthoukhong further down the road with 1,000-lb bombs by Strategic Airforce Liberator bombers in early May. Artillery shelling of Japanese positions followed, as did combined infantry and armour assaults, of which there were several. But Japanese resistance was stiff. Moreover, unlike in some of the other sectors at Imphal, the Japanese here were armed with anti-tank weapons. In one aborted British assault, several tanks were destroyed or damaged.

There was much fighting in May 1944 on the northern and southern banks of the turel (stream or river) which bisected the village. The area around the turel to the east of the bridge on the Tiddim Road was a particular focus. The bridge over the turel had been destroyed as the Japanese withdrew into South Potsangbam in the face of the 17th Indian Division's assaults. It was finally an operation from 10 to 15 May by the two Gurkha battalions of the 63rd Indian Brigade, with the support of tanks from the 3rd Carabiniers, which wrested the area around the bridge from the Japanese. But it had all taken a long time. The Japanese defence at Potsangbam had delayed the 17th Indian Division's 'hammer', following which it was decided to attack the Japanese in the hills to the west and force them south.

Potsangbam today is much larger than what it was in 1944. But fortunately, there are parts where one can still get a good sense of the vegetation and terrain in which the fighting had unfolded. Perhaps the best such place is the area of the Potsangbam turel to the immediate east of the bridge over the Tiddim Road. This is still not very built up today and one can walk and explore the northern bank of the turel. Dense bamboo clumps and foliage can still be found here and one can immediately see how they would have been exploited by the Japanese for their defence. And, in turn, how this would have made the task harder for the 17th Indian Division.

After Potsangbam, and before you reach the next major town, it is worth stopping by the side of the road and taking in the panorama from one of the paddy fields to the west. It is from here that one gets a proper perspective of the overall fighting in this sector. In the distance is the western hill range, which had been used as an approach route for at least two Japanese regiments (or brigades). The highest peak is clearly visible: this was what the British called Point 5846; it towers over Bishenpur and just above the Silchar Track as it crosses the hill range. One can also see from afar the sort of terrain this track traversed and in the vicinity of which two Victoria Crosses were won by men of the same unit on the same day—Naik Agan Singh Rai (referred to in war records as Agansing Rai) and Subadar Netra Bahadur Thapa (referred to in war records as Netrabahadur Thapa), both of the 2/5th Royal Gurkha Rifles, on 26 June 1944 (see Silchar Track box below). And finally, there are, all around, vistas of that mix of habitations and vegetation in the Imphal Valley that led some British veterans to describe the clashes there as 'village and paddy-field fighting'.

- Ningthoukhong

The next stop on the Tiddim Road is a bustling town that was a village in 1944: Ningthoukhong. As one passes through the main market today, at first glance it is hard to believe that this former village was one of the main Second World War battlefields in Manipur. But it is true: parts of Ningthoukhong were under Japanese control right through the battle in 1944 and saw nearly continuous fighting in that time. It was a key Japanese position in the Imphal Valley part of the Tiddim Road. Like at Potsangbam, the fulcrum of the fighting was the banks of the turel that divided the village into two halves. As the battle progressed, North Ningthoukhong came to be occupied by the British forces, while the Japanese were in South Ningthoukhong.

Ningthoukhong had been pattern bombed in May 1944, together with Potsangbam. Both sides also put in combined infantry and armour assaults during the battle, the Japanese for once having recourse to tanks of their own. Fighting was fierce and often at close quarters. Much of the village was destroyed in the hostilities at the time.

Ningthoukhong is very built up today and shows few signs of its Second World War past. Nevertheless, it is worth turning off the road and following the Ningthoukhong turel eastwards just before the—barely visible—bridge over it, for this neighbourhood and the banks of the turel were the scenes of such valour that for the visitor they are still hallowed ground as a battlefield. In fact, as you advance further along the stream, there are points where the houses fall away and the bamboo and trees close in and cling to the banks. It is here one must stop for a moment and ponder the military history associated with the area. Indeed, it was for their actions near the turel at Ningthoukhong in June 1944 that two men, Sergeant H.V. Turner of the 1st West Yorkshires and Rifleman Ganju Lama of the 1/7th Gurkha Rifles, were awarded the Victoria Cross.

Take Turner's story for instance. Sergeant Turner of the 1st West Yorkshires was posthumously awarded the Victoria Cross for his actions along the Ningthoukhong turel in the early hours of 7 June that year. He was one of the section commanders of the platoon that was defending a position by the turel targeted by the Japanese. He gathered a bag full of grenades and single-handedly went and attacked the approaching Japanese. He went back and forth on five occasions, each time collecting grenades and rushing off to attack the Japanese. On the sixth occasion, he was killed while throwing a grenade. Such are the scenes of fighting that were witnessed in these surroundings during the war.

Another case in point is Ningthoukhong Kha Khunou, a small village to the immediate south of Ningthoukhong on the Tiddim Road. It was an even smaller hamlet in 1944 and by mid-July it was where the Japanese were holding out to allow the withdrawal of their men from the hills to safety. In the early hours of 16 July, as part of a final push to clear the Japanese, some 9,000 artillery shells were fired on Ningthoukhong Kha Khunou. As one British veteran later wrote: 'It was one of the heaviest artillery concentrations yet fired in Burma.'[13] Today, it is a nondescript settlement that one barely notices as one moves down the road.

---

13 Grant, *Burma: The Turning Point*, p. 209.

The stream that flows through Ningthoukhong. Its banks were the scene of much fighting in 1944. Photo by Findlay Kember.

The area of the roadblock near Torbung. The hill in the background is Point 3404. Photo by Hemant Singh Katoch.

- Torbung

To get to Torbung, one must go past the fork in the road which leads to Moirang and continue down the Tiddim Road for several kilometres in the direction of Churachandpur. Just after the village of Torbung comes a point on the road where a couple of nullahs can be seen, with some hillocks alongside, east of the road. After Ningthoukhong this is yet another unremarkable landscape with yet another remarkable episode associated with it. It is this part of the road that was blocked by units of the 17th Indian Division as part their 'hammer and anvil' strategy of May 1944; indeed, the Torbung Roadblock from 17 to 24 May 1944 was the 'anvil' itself.

During that week, a roadblock was put up by the 48th Indian Brigade on the road, with its base on the hill called Point 3404 nearby. Established behind Japanese lines, the roadblock cut their main supply line at the time. And at a crucial moment. For this was when the White Tigers were planning their all-out assault on Bishenpur from the north, south and west. Men and materials destined to support that attack were prevented from moving up the road towards Bishenpur, thanks to the roadblock. As a result, it was frantically and repeatedly counterattacked by the Japanese for several days.

The roadblock was finally abandoned on May 24 after it became clear that the 'hammer' from the north would not materialize. The units responsible for the roadblock then made a fighting withdrawal up the road all the way to Potsangbam. Hundreds of Japanese soldiers are believed to have died in their attempts to pry open the roadblock. Today, it is only the nullahs off the road around which the roadblock had been set up that are de facto markers of the events of May 1944.

The Indian National Army Memorial Complex in Moirang.
Photo by Hemant Singh Katoch.

The spot where the INA raised its flag in April 1944.
Photo by Yaiphaba Meetei Kangjam.

- Moirang

The final stop in this sector is Moirang. The town lies on the southern edge of Loktak Lake. To get to it, you have to turn around from Torbung and head back up the road in the direction of Imphal. At the main fork in the road, the road turning off right (eastwards) must be taken for Moirang. In relation to the Second World War, it is here in Moirang that you find the INA Martyrs' Memorial complex, the only such extensive facility dedicated to the INA in the world.

The complex includes, among others, a war museum, an auditorium, a library, and a statue of Netaji Subhas Chandra Bose, the man who commanded the INA. For the longest time, this museum, which contains photos, relics of war and other artefacts, was the only Second World War museum in Manipur. The complex also contains two other sites of interest. One is the replica of the INA memorial at Singapore that had been blown up by the British after they had retaken the city in 1945.

The other is the spot because of which this complex is to be found at Moirang: the place where the INA is said to have first raised its flag after crossing over from Burma on 14 April 1944. This was done by men of the INA groups who came to the area along with the Japanese 33rd Division. Moirang was thus considered to be 'liberated' from British rule. There is also an old house on the outskirts of town that is believed to have served as the INA headquarters for the area.

Finally, Moirang is the main base for all visitors to Manipur to view and visit Loktak Lake, the largest freshwater lake in Northeast India. The Sendra Resort offers excellent views of the lake and near its entrance one can avail of boat rides on the lake too. For those interested, the Keibul Lamjao National Park, dubbed the only floating national park in the world, is also a short drive away.

The building in Moirang believed to have served as the INA's Manipur headquarters during the Imphal battle. Photo by Yaiphaba Meetei Kangjam.

Loktak Lake. Photo by Hemant Singh Katoch.

Point 5846 and the Silchar Track

The track between Bishenpur and Silchar (or, as it is locally known, the Old Cachar Road or Tongjei Maril) was never a major supply route to Imphal during the Second World War. That role was played by the Imphal–Kohima–Dimapur Road. The Silchar Track was indeed not much more than a track and its description as being 'Jeepable in dry season' in some of the war-era maps aptly summed up its condition. But the Japanese left nothing to chance in 1944. After cutting the Imphal–Kohima Road at the end of March, they sent a raiding party, which included some INA men, to cut the Silchar Track as well. This was done on the night of 14–15 April when a bridge on the track was blown up beyond the western hill range that overlooked the Imphal Valley. The siege of Imphal was complete.

The part of the Silchar Track that was of most relevance to the Imphal battle was the stretch from its starting point at Bishenpur to where it crosses the top of the western hill range. It is on and around these few miles of wriggling track where the Japanese and the British forces fought hard in 1944. The Japanese, who had their main column advancing on the ridgeline of the western hills, sought to prevent the British from using the track and to secure a corridor to supply their own units to the north (for their eventual advance to Imphal). On their part, the British tried to keep this part of the track open, both to prevent the Japanese from using it and to foil their attempts to gain a corridor across it.

These competing objectives resulted in months-long fighting for control of the Silchar Track. There were two particular areas of focus. The first was where the track crossed over the western hill range and the hills on either side of it there. This included Point 5846, the dramatic peak overlooking the track from the north and around which it curled, and the lesser hills to the south called Wooded Ridge (or Mori to the Japanese) and Wireless Hill (Antenna to the Japanese). Whoever held these hills had control over a vital part of the track and a commanding position over the entire area, including Bishenpur. In mid-April

1944 both sides raced to capture these hills and the British just about beat the Japanese to it.

The second area of contention was a series of bluffs and heights around the track that overlooked it as it wound its way up to Point 5846. To secure the route the British established piquets on these heights. These small positions were much fought over in 1944. Hand-to-hand fighting took place for possession of these positions with names such as Marne, Scrub, Water Piquet and Mortar Bluff. In fact, it was in the struggle for the latter two positions in the last week of June 1944 that two Victoria Crosses were won (see the box for Netra Bahadur Thapa's Victoria Cross citation). The guns at Bishenpur provided artillery support to the Fourteenth Army's infantry units in the area and tanks were brought up the treacherous track too to assist in operations. It was campaigning at its toughest, where it was often difficult to distinguish friend from foe in the hilly and jungle terrain.

Today, there are two ways to explore the Silchar Track. The first is to travel up the track itself from Bishenpur to just below Point 5846 (or Laimaton, as it is locally known). The advantage of this is that you are travelling on the original track most of the way, except close to Point 5846, where the present track takes a gentler gradient around. Part of the old alignment still survives and branches off to the right. There is thus the thrill of experiencing the original track of 1944 lore. However, the disadvantage of this approach can be the condition of the track itself, which can sometimes be in poor shape, especially during the rains. Given the still significant amount of foliage in the area and its relative isolation, it is also not easy to pinpoint the exact locations of the old piquets overlooking the track.

A more interesting—but strenuous—way to experience the area is via a trek along the ridgeline from the village of Lamdan to the south. To get to Lamdan, one has to turn off the Tiddim Road just short of Ningthoukhong and head up to the hills. The Manipur Mountaineering and Trekking Association (MMTA) has a facility at Lamdan and their trained guides can be availed for a trek from Lamdan northwards all the way up to the top of Point 5846.

For those who are fit enough to do this moderate trek, there are several plus points. For one, you are following in the footsteps of thousands of Japanese soldiers who had used the same route in these very hills in 1944. Second, on clear days there are terrific views to be had on all sides, which allow one to better understand the topography of this entire south-western sector of the Imphal battle. Third, en route you pass by the old battlefields of Dome, Wooded Hill and Wireless Hill, and the original alignment of the track under Point 5846. If you look around the track carefully enough, you will spot the remains of bunkers and dugouts that date back to the war. There is then the final ascent up Point 5846 itself, which involves clambering up a steep slope, with sharp drops on the sides.

It all makes for a terrific experience. Indeed, nothing brings home to you the nuances and intricacies of these battlefields than walking them yourself. For that is when you can even begin to comprehend veterans' accounts and the conditions men on all sides faced: the unexpected cold and mists, the leeches, the diarrhoea and dysentery, the inhospitable terrain, the sense of isolation and, of course, the formidable foes in 1944.

The Silchar–Bishenpur Track (or simply the Silchar Track) seen here heading west from Bishenpur. Photo by Hemant Singh Katoch.

Point 5846 (or Laimaton). Photo by Findlay Kember.

VC citation for Subadar Netra Bahadur Thapa

Subadar Netrabahadur Thapa was in command of the garrison of 41 men of the 2/5th Royal Gurkha Rifles (Frontier Force) which on the afternoon of 25th June, 1944, took over the isolated piquet known as Mortar Bluff situated on the hillside commanding the base at Bishenpur in Burma. The piquet position, completely devoid of any cover, was situated some 400 yards from the next piquet, from which it could be supported to some extent by 3-inch mortar fire, but was commanded by Water Piquet, a short distance away on high ground to the south, which had been overrun by strong enemy forces on the previous night and was still in enemy hands. Owing to its commanding position the retention of Mortar Bluff was vital to the safety of other positions farther down the ridge and to Bishenpur itself.

The relief had been harassed by enemy snipers at close range but was completed at 1830 hours without casualties. A little more than an hour later the enemy began to attack. For this purpose, a 75-millimetre and a 37-millimetre gun were brought on up to the high ground overlooking the position and poured shell after shell at point blank range for ten minutes into the narrow confines of the piquet, and this was followed by a determined attack by not less than one company of Japanese. A fierce fight ensued in which Subadar Netrabahadur Thapa's men, exhorted by their leader, held their ground against heavy odds and drove the enemy back with disproportionate losses. During this time Subadar Netrabahadur Thapa with tireless energy and contempt for his own safety moved from post to post encouraging his young NCOs and riflemen, of which the garrison was largely composed, and tending the wounded.

A short lull followed during which Subadar Netrabahadur Thapa gave a clear and concise report on the telephone to his Commanding Officer and asked for more artillery defensive fire. Having done this he made preparations to meet the next onslaught which was not long in coming.

Under cover of the pitch dark night and torrential rain the enemy had moved round to the jungle from the cover of which they launched their next attack. Still in considerable strength and as determined and ferocious as ever the enemy poured out from the jungle across the short space of open ground to the piquet defences under cover of small arms and 37-millimetre gun fire from a flank. For a time our men held their ground until, as ill-luck would have it, both the LMG and TMG of one section jammed.

With much reduced fire-power the section was unable to hold on, and the enemy forced an entrance and overran this and another section, killing or wounding 12 out of the 16 men comprising the two sections. Having no reserve Subadar Netrabahadur Thapa himself went forward from his Headquarters and stemmed any further advance with grenades.

The situation was however critical. With more than half his men casualties, ammunition low, and the enemy in possession of part of his perimeter, Subadar Netrabahadur Thapa would have been justified in withdrawing, but in his next report to his Commanding Officer he stated that he intended holding on and asked for reinforcements and more ammunition.

So efficient were his plans for defence and such was the fine example of this gallant Gurkha officer that not a man moved from his trench and not a yard more ground was gained by the enemy, despite their desperate attempts.

Thus the night passed until at 0400 hours a section of 8 men with grenades and small arms ammunition arrived. Their arrival inevitably drew fire and all the 8 were soon casualties. Undismayed, however, Subadar Netrabahadur Thapa retrieved the ammunition himself and with his platoon Headquarters took the offensive armed with grenades and khukris. Whilst so doing he received a bullet wound in the mouth followed shortly afterwards by a grenade which killed him outright. His body was found next day, khukri in hand and a dead Japanese with a cleft skull by his side.

True to the traditions of the service and his race Subadar Netrabahadur Thapa had fought against overwhelming odds for 8 hours before he was killed. His fine example of personal bravery and his high sense of duty so inspired his men that a vital position was held to the limit of human endurance. His valour and devotion to duty will remain an epic in the history of the Regiment.[14]

---

14 Supplement to the *London Gazette*, 10 October 1944.

Looking south from Point 5846 towards the positions Wooded Ridge, Wireless Hill, Dome (in the distance) and the western hills.
Photo by Hemant Singh Katoch.

Looking west from Point 5846 in the direction of Silchar.
Photo by Findlay Kember.

IMPHAL–KOHIMA, 1944   79

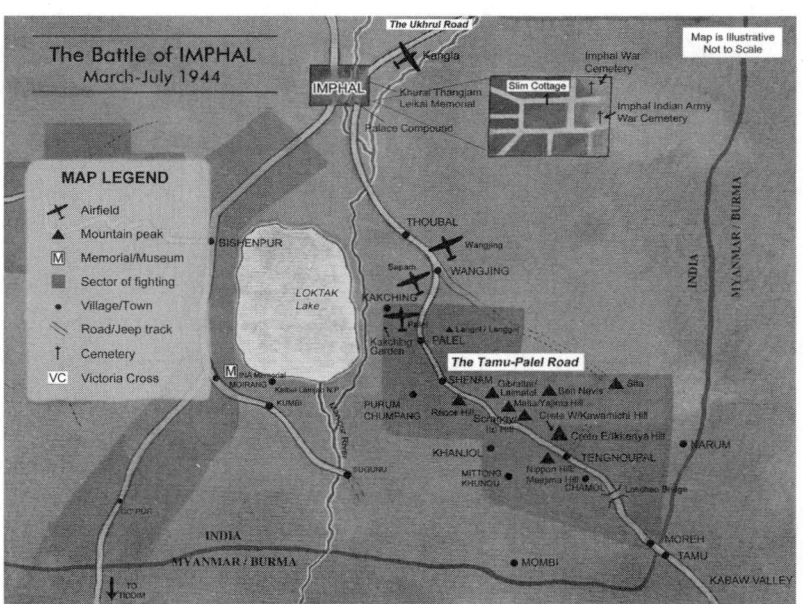

The Tamu–Palel Road and the Shenam Saddle
Courtesy of Robin Wahengbam, Hemant Singh Katoch and
Hemam Bishwajeet Singh.

3. The Tamu–Palel Road and the Shenam Saddle

> 'They are hills unknown to the outside world, but they will remain always in the memories of those who fought there. They were the scene of some of the most ferocious fighting of the whole war, and hundreds and hundreds of British, Indian, Gurkha and Japanese soldiers lost their lives on these hills which changed hands time and again as counter-attack followed attack.'[15]
>
> —Antony Brett-James and Geoffrey Evans, *Imphal, A Flower on Lofty Heights*

Battle narrative

The road connecting Tamu in Burma to Palel, or Pallel, in Manipur, then called the Tamu–Palel Road, was the main route into the Imphal Valley from across the frontier. In fact, this road, which crossed the mountains that run along the border, was *the* main route between India and Burma during the Second World War (and remains so today). Once it descends to Palel, it cuts right across the valley and enters Imphal from the south-east. As the Japanese planned their offensive in 1944, the Tamu–Palel Road was the obvious and natural choice for their approach to Imphal from this direction.

A key area on this road was what the British called the Shenam Saddle or Shenam Pass. This was a collection of hills—some have described it as one long ridge—at the highest point of the road, through and around which it snaked before it descended to Palel or Tamu (depending on where one was coming from). Some of the hills that made up the saddle were given names inspired by the Mediterranean, including Gibraltar, Malta, Cyprus, and Crete East and West. The Japanese would later refer to some of the hills by

---

15 Brett-James and Evans, *Imphal*, p. 230.

the names of officers who had captured them, including Maejima, Ikkenya and Kawamichi. Put simply, if the Japanese wanted to get to the Imphal Valley via this road, they had to get past the Shenam Saddle.

Deployed around Tamu was the 20th Indian Division under the command of Major General Douglas Gracey. Once the Japanese offensive got under way, his division was to withdraw to and up the road to make its stand on this approach to Imphal from the south-east. While the Shenam Saddle was to be one of the division's defensive positions, it was Moreh, then a village, the last on the road on the Indian side, which was to be the frontline position. As the Japanese attacked in mid-March 1944, the 20th Indian Division began its controlled withdrawal. But as it turned out, with the unexpected and growing Japanese threat to 4 Corps from the north-east, one of Gracey's brigades was sent back to the Imphal Valley to bolster its defences. Moreh was abandoned and the Shenam Saddle thus became the frontline British defensive position on the Tamu–Palel Road.

The Fourteenth Army units faced off here with Yamamoto Force. This was formed around an infantry group from the 33rd Division commanded by Major General Yamamoto. It had in support the 14th Tank Regiment and heavy and medium artillery guns; some described it as the Japanese formation with the best firepower at the outset of the campaign. Also present in the area was the INA. In fact, this was where the INA was concentrated in the Imphal battle: some 6,000 men from its 1st Division were deployed on the flanks of Yamamoto Force off the Tamu–Palel Road.

The fighting in this sector involved repeated Japanese attempts to get past the 20th Indian Division's defences on the Shenam Saddle. From mid-May 1944 onwards, the 23rd Indian Division took its place. The main body of Yamamoto Force attacked the hills that made up the Shenam Saddle position on the Tamu–Palel Road. They managed to capture some ground, positions were won and lost, but the Japanese were never able to overwhelm their opponents. The British, Indian and Gurkha units put up strong resistance and managed to prevent the Japanese from proceeding towards Imphal down this road.

As the battle progressed, the Japanese sought to bypass the saddle by sending units through the hills to the north (via places such as Langol {or Langgol}), while a group of INA soldiers tried to do the same from the south. These efforts were also ultimately rebuffed. Yamamoto Force retained its presence on the saddle through the 1944 battle; it was evicted only in the last week of July after the Fourteenth Army launched its final counterattack in the area.

Battlefield guide

Those who have the time and are willing to brave a journey of approximately three–four hours each way, punctuated by multiple military checkposts, they can go all the way to the border town of Moreh, and then head back to Imphal. But this guide suggests a day-long tour which involves going up to the Shenam Saddle and returning to Imphal the same day. This is more manageable and comfortable, and avoids the main checkposts on the road.

Heading south-east out of Imphal on what is called the Moreh Road today, you travel in the valley through countryside similar to that found along the Tiddim Road: towns and villages, separated by paddy fields, with the hills in the distance. The road is quite busy until the town of Thoubal, after which the population density decreases on the stretch to Palel. In the paddy fields east of the road just before the town of Wangjing, there used to be the fair-weather Wangjing Airfield in 1944.

Another such airfield, Sapam, was in the paddy fields west of the road between Wangjing and the turnoff (Kakching Lamkhai) for Kakching town, but well short of the turnoff. These were among the multiple airfields that had come up in the valley during the Second World War. The two fair-weather strips had been carved out of the paddy fields at the time. There is little obvious trace of them today: the villagers have long since reclaimed their lands and they have rightly reverted to being what they had always been but for the interruption of the war—paddy fields.

- Palel Airfield

The first stop on the tour involves a view of what was the third airfield in this sector: Palel. Unlike Wangjing and Sapam, Palel was an all-weather airfield. Being only the second of its kind in the valley besides Imphal Main, it was important to the overall defence of Imphal. It assumed even greater importance due to the supply dumps and other military support facilities around the airfield. Palel Airfield was, therefore, a key target for Yamamoto Force and one which seemed eminently attainable. Indeed, on a clear day one could spot the airfield in the distance from some of the peaks of the Shenam Saddle.

The Japanese tried to reach the airfield from several directions in 1944. There was the push down the Tamu–Palel Road via the saddle. A group of some 300 INA soldiers were also sent to approach the airfield from the south in early May (more on that below). But the most successful effort by the Japanese was through the hills north of the Tamu–Palel Road. On the night of 3–4 July, a small party managed to infiltrate the airfield and blew up eight parked aircraft. But that was to be the height of their achievements with regard to this airfield, which otherwise effectively played its role in supporting 4 Corps through the Imphal battle.

Perhaps of greater interest in India is the fate of the INA attack on Palel Airfield in early May 1944. This attack from the south was supposed to be coordinated with a Japanese assault from north of the Tamu–Palel Road. There are multiple accounts of what happened to the 300-strong INA force that closed in on the airfield from the south. One says they got right to the perimeter, while another says they reached within five miles of it. Either way, the INA men came up against their former comrades, the Gurkha and Indian soldiers of the Indian Army. Parleys aimed at trying to convince the latter to come over to the INA side were said to have been rejected and the INA group was subjected to fierce counterattacks.

It has been argued that the failure at Palel and, in particular, the counterattacks by Indian Army units on the INA was a major blow to the morale of some of the latter's soldiers. It brought home to them the extent of the animosity they attracted from within the ranks of the (British-led) Indian Army at the time. Some INA men did subsequently surrender; however, the greater majority chose to fight on. Of the around 6,000 men of the INA's 1st Division at Imphal, 2,600 returned, of which 2,000 had to be sent to hospital. Some 400 men were killed in the fighting, 715 men deserted, about 800 surrendered, and around 1,500 died of disease and starvation.[16]

The old Palel Airfield is now under the control of the Assam Rifles. The compound is today known as Kakching Garrison after the eponymous town next door. Only a part of the old runway remains; the rest has been built over and access is restricted. The best way to catch a glimpse of the old airfield and get a sense of its size is from the hillocks nearby. The popular tourist attraction of Kakching Garden

---

16 Hugh Toye, *Subhash Chandra Bose: The Springing Tiger*, (London: Cassell, 1959), p. 184.

on top of one such hillock provides a good vantage point for both the airfield and the surrounding area. After turning off the main road at Kakching Lamkhai, follow the signs for the garden.

Distant view of the old Palel Airfield from Kakching Garden, a popular tourist spot in Manipur today. Photo by Hemant Singh Katoch.

The Shenam Saddle or Shenam Pass. Seen here are parts of Recce Hill (foreground), Gibraltar (right), Malta (left) and the Tamu–Palel Road below. Photo by Findlay Kember.

- Tamu–Palel Road

Getting back on the main road, you quickly cross the town of Palel, which lent its name both to the airfield and to the road to Tamu in Burma. From here on the road starts its ascent, winding and twisting its way up the hills. The temperature starts to drop, as does the population density. The scenery becomes more dramatic, with vistas of green hills and ravines. It is a welcome relief from the relative heat of the valley.

There is an enormous amount of Second World War history associated with this road. It was through here that thousands of desperate refugees made their way into India after fleeing the advancing Japanese in Burma in 1942. This is also where the British retreat from Burma, the longest in its military history, ended in 1942. The Japanese would try and make their way down the very same road during their Imphal offensive two years later in 1944. Once they were defeated and chased back to Burma, this was again the road used by the victorious Fourteenth Army in the latter half of 1944 and in 1945 to pour into Central Burma and race towards Rangoon. If there is any road that encapsulates the title of Slim's book *Defeat into Victory*, this is it.

- Shenam Saddle

On the climb up you cross what is locally known as Sinam village; its anglicized form 'Shenam' is what the saddle ahead is named after. There is also a visible presence of Indian paramilitary forces en route. It serves as a reminder that one is just around 50 km away from the international border between India and Burma, and this area is considered militarily sensitive by the authorities.

It is around one of the bends in the road that you get your first view of the Shenam Saddle. It is quite a sight. For there lie these spectacular battlefields, a collection of quiet and desolate hills at an altitude of 5,000 feet, for the most part uninhabited and unchanged since the time of the Second World War. You are lucky if you get such a view, however: on many occasions these peaks are barely visible, covered as they are in thick fog and mist.

There are two ways to explore the Shenam Saddle. One is to start with the first major hill you encounter, Recce Hill, and then stop at or near every subsequent one as you go forward. The other option is to drive through the saddle—and then retrace your steps, stopping along the way. The author prefers the latter as it mirrors the Japanese advance on the saddle in 1944. Moreover, the preferred modus operandi is to not go all the way to Tengnoupal village, which lies at the eastern end of the saddle. Instead, one can stop just below the old battlefield of Scraggy, from where you get a good view of the old Nippon Hill and Crete—and, importantly, avoid what can sometimes become a long stop at a military checkpoint a short distance away. But if a visitor has the time and is not deterred by multiple checkpoints, one can drive all the way down to the town of Moreh on the border with Burma. This is a scenic route and you pass along the way other battlefields and sites of interest, such as the bridge over the Lokchao River that was the scene of much fighting in 1944.

- Nippon Hill

Driving through the saddle, you come to a stop on the road just beyond Scraggy. With your back to that hill, you can clearly see straight ahead in the near distance Nippon Hill and, to the left, parts of Crete. These features are clustered around the village of Tengnoupal on the road. It was from there in the east to Gibraltar on the western edge of the saddle, where the fighting was concentrated in 1944—a distance of just around 5 km.

Elements of Yamamoto Force managed to take the heights of Nippon Hill in the last week of March 1944 while the 20th Indian Division was still withdrawing up the road. The small number of Japanese could not exploit this early success, however, and the rest of the division completed its withdrawal by 4 April. In the first half of that month, there was much fighting for control of Nippon Hill. After initial, piecemeal attempts failed, it was left to the 1st Devonshire Regiment to launch a more concerted counterattack on April 11. Made with three companies, and supported by artillery and Hurribombers, this proved successful and Nippon Hill was back in British hands.

It had been a tough fight. But the Japanese had still not given up. They attempted repeated assaults and tried to recapture the hill. By 16 April, Nippon Hill was again with the Japanese. The British decided to refrain from trying to recover this hill again and it remained under Yamamoto Force's control until the end of the battle. The fight for Nippon Hill typified the sort of fighting that took place on the Shenam Saddle: hills exchanged hands as attack followed counterattack. The hill also highlighted the Japanese soldier's tenacity and his determination to defend. For it was here that he had dug himself in deep, creating a network of holes and passages from which it became very difficult to dislodge him. It was also at Nippon Hill where it was reported that days after it had been recaptured by the Devons, the odd Japanese soldier would emerge from the ground and—half-alive—try and attack.

Nippon Hill today is occupied by the Assam Rifles. From where you are standing under Scraggy, you can see why the Japanese struggled so hard to capture the hill. From Nippon Hill and the adjacent ridge you can look on to several of the features on the Shenam Saddle. The Japanese went on to station some of their guns there and their firing became a consistent nuisance to the defenders of the saddle.

To the left of Nippon Hill is Crete. This feature and Cyprus (which is hidden from view) were the next Japanese targets in 1944. Crete East and Cyprus were both taken by Yamamoto Force about a week after the fall of Nippon Hill. Crete West became the next in line.

- Crete West

Today Crete West is still largely uninhabited and covered in low vegetation. At the end of April and early May 1944, this feature was subjected to increasingly frantic attacks. The infantry made multiple assaults and there was intense firing by Japanese artillery guns. But the defenders of the 20th Indian Division clung on. The Japanese then bypassed Crete West and captured a smaller hill next to Scraggy called Lynch on 8 May. The defenders of Crete West were isolated and a couple of days later they had to fall back to Scraggy. This small hill then became the frontline between the British and the Japanese forces on the Shenam Saddle.

View of Scraggy straight ahead, Nippon Hill on the right and a part of Malta on the left. Photo by Hemant Singh Katoch.

Remains of trenches on Recce Hill. Photo by Hemant Singh Katoch.

- Scraggy

Scraggy is arguably the most iconic battlefield of the Imphal battle. It is the fighting here between the Japanese, Britons, Gurkhas and Indians for weeks that has inspired comparisons with the Somme in the First World War and with Kohima. This is not without reason. The conditions were grim, with forward positions of both sides mere yards apart in places; there were trench raids and shelling and sniping from both sides, often from positions on Scraggy itself; the body parts of combatants lay strewn about in the churned-up soil; the stench of death hung low on the hillside; and the incessant rains later in the battle made an already miserable situation infinitely worse. It was a truly horrific scene of battle.

The first major Japanese assault on Scraggy came on the night of 10 May. Literally wave upon wave of infantry charged on to the hill. The situation became so desperate that the British infantry commander had to call for artillery fire on his own forward positions to try and stop the Japanese onslaught. By the next morning, the Japanese were found to be in possession of parts of the hill, which they were to then hang on to—much like Nippon Hill—right until the end of the Imphal battle in July 1944. It came at quite a cost: by one estimate, several hundred Japanese are believed to have died in this first attack on Scraggy alone.

Multiple other attacks followed in the next two months as Yamamoto Force sought desperately to break through and capture the rest of Scraggy. A major one came some ten days after the first attack on Scraggy, but this was foiled. Another full-scale attack was launched on the night of 9–10 June. There was heavy shelling, followed by infantry assaults. This time the Japanese were able to overwhelm the defenders—soldiers of the 23rd Indian Division by then—and take the crest of Scraggy. A massive counterattack was soon put in, which included artillery concentrations, airstrikes and a fightback by two units of Gurkhas. But the Japanese held Scraggy's crest and they were left to stay in place. They were evicted only when the final British push to clear the Shenam Saddle took place at the end of July.

All of the above seems quite extraordinary to consider if you visit Scraggy today. It is an unremarkable-looking hill and is overgrown with thick bushes, small trees and low-lying vegetation, something which makes exploring it surprisingly difficult. It is also very quiet, a far cry from what it was like at the time of the war. One can only be grateful that Scraggy still lies here relatively untouched and isolated, for it allows one to appreciate the feature and contemplate the dramatic events it was witness to in 1944.

- Gibraltar

Moving back from Scraggy, you pass by the much larger hill of Malta. Together with Gibraltar, these were the three peaks that made up the bulwark of the Shenam Saddle defences. Subjected to regular shelling from the Japanese, life was also difficult for the troops deployed on this hill, although perhaps it was relatively more bearable than the experience at Scraggy. It was at the more precipitous feature (over 5,100 feet high) of Gibraltar next to it, however, where for a brief moment it seemed that the Japanese would be able to break through to the Imphal Valley.

In the second half of May 1944, the Japanese made several attacks against Gibraltar. These were beaten back. But in the early hours of 24 May, they managed to capture its peak. That morning, the defenders of the Shenam Saddle were stunned to see the Japanese flag fluttering high on Gibraltar. With the fall of Gibraltar, Malta and the part of Scraggy under the 23rd Indian Division's control had been left isolated. If this hill was not swiftly recovered, the entire defensive position on the saddle was at risk of being lost.

Immediate counterattacks were ordered that morning. The Japanese positions on Gibraltar were heavily shelled first. The much harder task of evicting them was left to the 5/6th Rajputana Rifles and the 3/10th Gurkhas. The former made some progress and recaptured some of the ground lost. It was finally the Gurkhas who clambered up the final narrow ridge—only two men abreast could pass through—and stormed the crest in a dramatic khukri charge. The Japanese on the reverse slope had resisted these moves with grenade attacks and machine gun fire, but they were finally overcome. Some 145 Japanese bodies were found on Gibraltar, while many others fled the final assault, a rare sight during the Imphal battle.

Like Scraggy, Gibraltar today also seems unchanged from the Second World War. It towers over the road and it is only when you try to climb its lower slopes do you realize just how steep it is. If merely climbing it is this difficult today, one cannot even imagine what it must have been like when a full-fledged battle took place for it in May 1944.

- Recce Hill

The final stop on the Shenam Saddle is what was known as Recce Hill. The highest feature on the saddle, it was at a relatively safe distance from the worst of the fighting in the area. It is today the most accessible of the hills on the saddle. After informing the small post of the Manipur Rifles on the road at its base, you can climb right up to the top of Recce Hill.

The hill is notable for two main reasons. One, it still has what can only be described as perhaps the best preserved and most extensive network of bunkers, trenches and dugouts from 1944. These weave over and around the sprawling feature and can be easily spotted. Nothing compares to walking and exploring these reminders of the Second World War in such dramatic surroundings.

And that is the second point: on a clear day Recce Hill affords the most stunning views possible of the entire area. It is when you gaze at Gibraltar, Malta and Nippon Hill in the distance, with the Tamu–Palel Road running through, that the words that follow ring ever so true. They are of a British veteran, John Hudson, who was deployed on the Shenam Saddle in 1944: 'How strange that such a vast area of mountains and jungle along the frontier between India and Burma lay undisturbed, whilst we beat the hell out of each other on this one small patch.'[17]

---

17 John Hudson, *Sunset in the East* (Barnsley: Pen and Sword, 2002), p. 73.

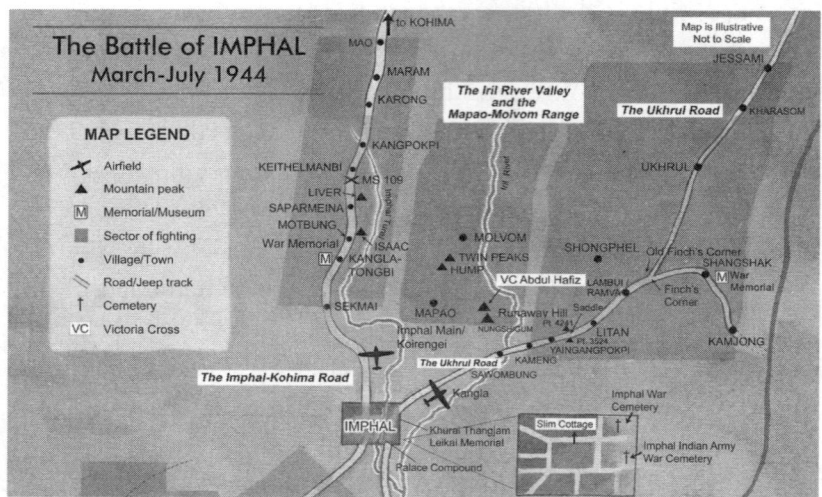

The Ukhrul Road, the Iril River Valley and the Imphal–Kohima Road
Courtesy of Robin Wahengbam, Hemant Singh Katoch and
Hemam Bishwajeet Singh.

4. The Ukhrul Road and the Iril River Valley

'Ukhrul was the rallying point for the Japanese 15th and 31st Divisions and for all detachments and stragglers, east and north of Imphal.'[18]

—Field Marshal Viscount Slim, *Defeat into Victory*

Battle narrative

The British were expecting the Japanese to come up the two roads from the south: the Tiddim Road and the Tamu–Palel Road. These were the obvious routes of invasion from Burma. Where they were not expecting Mutaguchi to send troops in great strength was from the north of Imphal. The assumption was that at most a Japanese regiment (brigade) would be pushed through this vast region of high mountains and limited road infrastructure. Its likely aim would be to cut the vital supply line of the Imphal–Kohima–Dimapur Road, probably at Kohima. It is to Mutaguchi's credit then that in March 1944 he directed the most powerful of his thrusts in Burma from the direction in which it was least expected. Two infantry divisions, the 15th Division and the 31st Division, crossed the Chindwin River and made their way towards Imphal and Kohima respectively from here.

The area around Ukhrul and Shangshak (or Sangshak, as it is referred to in war memoirs) lay en route to Imphal and Kohima and was thus important to the movement of these Japanese troops. Ukhrul lay in the zone of responsibility of the 31st Division, under the command of Lieutenant General Sato, whose target was Kohima. Shangshak, to its south, was within the northern limits of the zone under the charge of the 15th Division commanded by Lieutenant General Yamauchi, which aimed for Imphal.

---

18 Slim, *Defeat into Victory*, p. 400.

On the Fourteenth Army's side, the 23rd Indian Division, which was in reserve, was responsible for the Ukhrul region, including Shangshak. Its 49th Indian Brigade had been deployed there at the outset of the battle. Once the Japanese offensive began, however, even this formation was withdrawn. It was rushed south down the Tiddim Road to the assistance of the 17th Indian Division which had been cut off by Yanagida's men. Its place was hurriedly taken by the 50th Indian Parachute Brigade under the command of Brigadier Hope-Thomson. This parachute brigade had only just arrived in Imphal. The original plan was for it to be deployed to rear areas, more for active-service training and some patrolling, instead of immediate deployment for active combat with the Japanese.

But the 50th Indian Parachute Brigade would soon find itself facing a powerful column of the Japanese 31st Division, as well as units of the 15th Division. A crucial battle between the two sides would follow in Shangshak village in March 1944 (see Shangshak section below). By the end of it, although the entire area of Ukhrul and Shangshak would come under Japanese control, several of its units would be delayed in their advance on Imphal and Kohima.

After the withdrawal of the 50th Indian Parachute Brigade from Shangshak, men of the 5th Indian Division were rushed up to plug the gaps on this approach to Imphal. They had been flown in from the Arakan and immediately sent into battle. From around mid-April, the 23rd Indian Division would take over operations up the Ukhrul Road. In mid-May, they would switch places with Gracey's 20th Indian Division on the Shenam Saddle.

During the Imphal battle, the road from Imphal to Ukhrul (or the Ukhrul Road) and its vicinity would also be one of the 'spokes' used by the Japanese 15th Division to try and get to Imphal. But as was the case with the other spokes, Yamauchi's advance would be first met and halted, and then pushed back by the Fourteenth Army. While the reinforcements flown in from the Arakan (5th Indian Division) played a pivotal role in the former action, the latter was led by the 23rd Indian Division and then the 20th Indian Division. The push back in this sector involved fighting up the road to clear the Japanese present on and around it, as well as wide flanking movements to the left (north) and right (south) of the road.

The Ukhrul–Shangshak area would again assume importance towards the end of the twin battles of Imphal and Kohima as it would be through here that the survivors of the 15th and 31st Divisions would pass on their way back to Burma. In fact, Ukhrul would be among the last Japanese strongholds to fall in the battle, and would only be recaptured in early July 1944.

The valley of the Iril river was closely connected to events around the Ukhrul Road. The Japanese 15th Division was active there, as well. As the battle progressed in 1944, Fourteenth Army units undertook extensive patrolling and operations on both sides of the Iril river. These had multiple aims: to directly target the Japanese in the hills around the Iril River Valley; cut the east–west running supply lines in the area; help isolate the Japanese on the Mapao–Molvom Range and Imphal–Kohima Road (see next section); and support the opening of the Ukhrul Road itself.

Battlefield guide

This guide suggests a day-long tour that involves going north-east of Imphal up the Ukhrul Road. For a comfortable day out and given the road condition, you can go all the way to Shangshak, briefly stop by Ukhrul, and return to Imphal the same evening. This allows you to visit the main battlefields in the area and get a sense of the terrain in this sector.

- Kangla Airfield

Heading out of Imphal on the Ukhrul Road, the scenery opens up soon after you cross Lamlong Bazar. At this point if you look right, the paddy fields to the immediate east of the road were once Kangla Airfield. This was another of the fair-weather airfields in the valley during the Second World War, similar to Wangjing and Sapam. Except for the markings on maps which point out its general location, here too there is little visible sign among the paddy fields of the old airfield.

The paddy fields that were once the fair-weather Kangla Airfield along the Ukhrul Road. Photo by Hemant Singh Katoch.

The heights of Nungshigum visible from Keibi village. Pyramid is to the left; Southern Bump is in the centre; and Northern Bump is to the right. Photo by Hemant Singh Katoch.

- Nungshigum

As you continue on the road, you can see in the distance to the northwest spurs of the feature the British called Nungshigum in 1944. To get a sense of the full scale of this sprawling massif, you have to get off the Ukhrul Road at Sawombung—that is, go straight towards Keibi village at the point where the main road curves right. You are now roughly following the trajectory of the Iril river, which flows to the east of this lesser country road. To your left loom the many spurs and the main massif of Nungshigum.

The Japanese knew Nungshigum as Hill 3833, a reference to the height in feet of its highest point. The British also had names for its peaks—Southern Bump (or Twin Bumps), its highest point, which was distinct from Northern Bump, its slightly lower northern peak. The hill was an attractive target to the Japanese: it was a short distance away from Imphal Main Airfield and 4 Corps headquarters and within striking distance of both Kangla Airfield and the outskirts of Imphal. And so at the end of the first week of April 1944, during the crucial opening stage of the battle when Imphal was at its most vulnerable, a battalion of the Japanese 51st Regiment (15th Division) attacked Nungshigum.

The fight for Nungshigum lasted a week. After see-saw clashes between the Japanese and the 3/9th Jats (5th Indian Division), by 11 April the former were firmly installed on its heights. Because of the location of Nungshigum, this was an unacceptable risk to the defence of Imphal. The British were determined to remove this proximate threat to 4 Corps and put in an overwhelming counterattack on 13 April. This involved the infantry (two companies of the 1/17th Dogras), artillery (the 5th Indian Division's guns), air force (three squadrons of Vengeance dive bombers and Hurribombers) and, in an inspired move, armour. The latter consisted of a squadron of the 3rd Carabiniers sent up the slopes together with the infantry, with another squadron and the artillery positioned on either side of the massif.

The operation began with the strafing and aerial bombardment of the Japanese positions on the heights of Nungshigum. The guns and armour on the plain fired next, after which the infantry and tanks on the feature itself moved in to finish the job at close quarters. The Japanese put up a fierce fight. But the deployment of the Lee/Grant tanks up the slopes of Nungshigum proved decisive. The Japanese never expected to encounter tanks at such a height and were not armed to counter them. Their defences on the Southern and Northern Bumps were eventually overcome later that day, with the tanks playing a decisive role in taking the Japanese bunkers.

Some 250 bodies of Japanese soldiers were later recovered from Nungshigum. But the operation had also proven costly to the victors: all of the British tank officers were killed and both infantry company commanders were injured. The former had had to stick their head out of their tanks' turrets to safely guide their machines on the narrow ridge on Nungshigum, which had made them easy targets for Japanese snipers and fire. It had finally been left to the Viceroy's Commissioned Officer (VCO) of the Dogras, Subadar Ranbir Singh, and Squadron Sergeant-Major Craddock of the Carabiniers to press ahead and conclude the battle that day.

Nungshigum was the closest the Japanese would come to Imphal as an organized force in 1944. As such, it is the battlefield closest to Imphal. The feature lies largely unchanged from the time of the war: it is devoid of human settlement and its heights and slopes are covered in a mix of small trees, bushes and other vegetation. You can get a good sense of its heights and the ridge connecting them—which the tanks had traversed in single file—from the Keibi village side of the hill (to its east). From here one can also see the hills east of the Iril river to which the Japanese at Nungshigum had withdrawn after their defeat in the battle.

If you approach Nungshigum from the west (via the Pangei Road), you can see to its immediate north-west the small hill the

British called Runaway Hill. It is said that it had been so named because of the rare sight of the Japanese running away from that hill in the face of a determined assault on it by Jemadar Abdul Hafiz of the 3/9th Jats. The hill had been lost to the Japanese as part of their advance on Nungshigum. Hafiz had led the effort to recover the hill on 6 April, which he did with extreme bravery and in the face of intense Japanese fire. He was killed in this action, for which he was posthumously awarded the Victoria Cross; it is claimed that he was the first Muslim recipient of this award in the Second World War.

Runaway Hill. Photo by Hemant Singh Katoch.

View of the Ukhrul Road as it approaches the hill (on the right) near Kameng that the Japanese attacked in April 1944. Photo by Hemant Singh Katoch.

- Kameng

Getting back on to the Ukhrul Road, the next place of interest is near Lamlai where the hills on both sides close in, leaving a gap of just a couple of thousand yards through which the road passes. After the British withdrawal from Shangshak at the end of March, this became the major defensive position on the Ukhrul Road. There was concern that the Japanese would come down this way and so for a period the entire gap was ringed and fortified by barbed wire. Positions were established on the hills on the left (north) and right (south) of the road. These came under attack in early April as the Japanese 15th Division sought to break through.

Much has been written about the attack on the position south of the road near the village of Kameng in the early hours of 4 April. One Japanese company attacked the hill manned by the 1/17th Dogras. But it was a foolhardy effort: most of those who survived the concentrated fire from the defenders would subsequently face shelling by the artillery and tanks. A hundred bodies were later found here and very few Japanese made it back alive. The hill near Kameng can clearly be seen from the road today and you can climb up a bit of the way to get a sense of the hills nearby, including Point 4057, which lies to the immediate north of the road. The Japanese attack on that position had also been repulsed by mid-April.

- Saddle

The road continues on in nearly a straight line, cutting through paddy fields until Gwaltabi. The hills begin from this village and the road climbs up until it reaches a saddle before twisting its way down towards the bridge over the Thoubal River at Litan. Called Mahadev today, this point was known as the Saddle position in 1944. To its north lay the feature called Point 4241, while to its south lay Point 3524. Saddle first came under Japanese control after the British withdrawal from the area at the end of March. It was recaptured a couple of weeks later in mid-April by the 23rd Indian Division.

Once the 20th Indian Division arrived in mid-May, it was from the Saddle area that the long, difficult slog to clear the Japanese further up the Ukhrul Road began. Not only was this effort strongly resisted, it was around Saddle where the Japanese put in surprisingly strong attacks in June. Their infantry was supported by machine gun and artillery fire, and managed to capture some ground on both Point 4241 and Point 3524. The attacks were carried out by units of the 15th Division and came at a time when the Japanese were otherwise largely on the defensive in this sector. This was a last-gasp effort by the Japanese in the Saddle area, however; as elsewhere, the positions were recovered and the slow but steady effort to clear the road continued.

The best way to get a sense of the Saddle position is to view it from the valley (after you cross Lamlai), before you start climbing up the road. You can then clearly make out the saddle-like shape of the position, flanked by Point 4241 and Point 3524. From the old Saddle itself today, there are terrific views over the Imphal Valley. Standing there you immediately understand the importance of its location: from here a force could proceed relatively unimpeded all the way down to Kameng. In the opposite direction, it could serve as a springboard to advance speedily down to Litan and beyond.

The position called Saddle on the Ukhrul Road in the distance. Flanking it are the features called Point 4241 (on the left) and Point 3524 (on the right). Photo by Hemant Singh Katoch.

The old stone marker for Finch Corner. Photo by Findlay Kember.

- Finch Corner

Carrying on down the road, you cross the Thoubal River at Litan. The village is surrounded by high mountains and was deemed indefensible by a British commanding officer in 1944. It was attacked and taken over by the Japanese in March and was later the scene of clashes as the British forces fought to clear the road. In fact, it was at Litan where two brigades of the 23rd Indian Division—before its departure for the Shenam Saddle—coming from opposite directions had linked up on 22 April.

It should be noted that from Litan to Finch Corner (and from there to Ukhrul), some stretches of the road you travel on are not the same as those that existed at the time of the Imphal battle. The alignment has since been changed in favour of gentler gradients. The villages near the present-day road up to Finch Corner, including Shokvao (referred to as Sokpao in some war accounts), T.M. Kasom (referred to as Kasom) and Lambui (referred to as Lamu or Lammu), all saw fierce fighting in 1944. For instance, in April the Shokvao–T.M. Kasom area was where Lieutenant General Yamauchi's headquarters was believed to be, and it came under attack from units of the 23rd Indian Division (he escaped). In early July, as the final push was made to open the road towards Ukhrul, it was in the present-day Lambui–Ramva area where Japanese resistance was the stiffest.

The next stop on the road, after some breathtaking scenery to the right, is Finch Corner. This is the name given to the junction on the Ukhrul Road: the fork to the right leads to Shangshak and beyond, while the road to the left leads to Ukhrul and farther north. The junction is named after a British Major Finch who first constructed the road during the Second World War. But this is not the original Finch Corner. That can be found just short of its present-day location, up a dirt path that branches off sharply to the left.

After a few hundred yards you come to the original location of Finch Corner, easily identifiable by a stone marker dating back to the Second World War. You can still see the original road from Imphal to that junction today, with the two old forks—all dirt tracks today—branching off around the historic stone marker. Parts of the inscription on the marker are still legible today, including a Biblical quotation. It is a truly atmospheric spot.

Looking on to what was the main British defensive position at Shangshak village (Sangshak) in March 1944. Photo by Hemant Singh Katoch.

View of Shangshak village from the east. Photo by Findlay Kember.

- Shangshak (Sangshak)

Going back down to the present-day Finch Corner, you take the right fork to go to Shangshak. As noted earlier, it was at this village—called Sangshak in war memoirs—that a battle took place in March 1944, which involved the 50th Indian Parachute Brigade and Japanese units making their way towards Kohima (mainly) and Imphal. Units of this brigade had only just arrived in the area when their forward positions reported seeing large numbers of Japanese heading in their direction. They belonged to the column of the 31st Division that was to make its way to Kohima via Ukhrul. Major General Miyazaki, the commander of this division's infantry group, was in charge.

The brigade's forward positions came under attack from the Japanese. Valiant efforts were nevertheless made to try and hold ground, such as at Point 7378 where a company held out on 19–20 March. But it was overwhelmed by the numerically far superior Japanese force, and it was soon decided to concentrate the 50th Indian Parachute Brigade at Shangshak. On the Japanese side, Miyazaki made a decision that has been debated ever since: he directed units of his 58th Regiment from Ukhrul towards Shangshak. But Miyazaki's men should never have been sent to Shangshak as it lay out of his area of responsibility—it was to be under Yamauchi's

15th Division. It is believed that once aware of the brigade's presence in the village, he had not wanted to leave such a large force to his rear as he made his way to Kohima.

And so, on 22 March a fierce battle began at Shangshak. The 50th Indian Parachute Brigade faced wave upon wave of Japanese infantry attacks over the next four days, many of which came from what was called West Hill. The former was concentrated in a position just a few hundred yards in length and width. The Britons, Indians and Gurkhas faced a desperate situation, devoid of reliable sources of water or barbed wire to ring their perimeter. Japanese artillery guns repeatedly fired on the crowded position, never lacking for targets. As the days and nights wore on, the defence of Shangshak village became increasingly untenable. Matters were not helped when some units of the Japanese 15th Division also joined the attack towards the end.

Finally, on the night of 26 March, the defenders of Shangshak were given the go-ahead to withdraw towards Imphal. Although the Japanese took the village, they had paid a high price. Estimates of Japanese casualties go up to as high as 1,000 and several company commanders were lost. Of great import was the fact that the Japanese had been delayed in their march towards Kohima and Imphal. Coming as this delay did at the beginning of the offensive, it provided valuable time to the Fourteenth Army to shore up its defences.

Shangshak today is an interesting battlefield to explore. You can start with the football field that was already in existence in 1944 and across which the Japanese had launched some of their attacks. To the left is the old West Hill position, atop which a modern church now stands; to the right is the old British defensive position. Of course, today the village is larger than it was in 1944 and these old battlefields have houses on them. It is nevertheless a charming village to explore and you can broadly make out where the old positions were.

In fact, you can walk through the village and cover the main areas of the fighting, including the north-western corner of the old position where the old church stood in 1944 (it has since been moved). This part of the village saw some of the worst of the fighting. A Japanese account noted: 'Hand-to-hand fighting was everywhere and hand grenades flew everywhere. Our comrades encouraged us, the enemy screamed at us. Thus the top of the hill turned to a hell on earth.'[19]

What makes Shangshak even more special are the shallow trenches that can still be found in the undergrowth and the forest on the edge of the village, towards the east. You can ask a local to show them to you, an experience that vividly brings the past to life. Shangshak is also home to a war memorial dedicated to the 1944 battle. It has been constructed by the Indian Army and is maintained by the Assam Rifles. Nearby is another, private, memorial in the residential compound of a survivor of the Second World War. All of these serve to remind us of this little village's extraordinary wartime experience.

Remains of trenches dating back to the Second World War around Shangshak village. Photo by Findlay Kember.

---

19 Harry Seaman, *The Battle at Sangshak* (London: Leo Cooper, 1989), p. 96.

The war memorial that commemorates the Shangshak (Sangshak) battle. Photo by Findlay Kember.

- Ukhrul

The last stop in the area is present-day Ukhrul town. Ukhrul remained under Japanese control right through the battle in 1944. As noted earlier, it was through here that many of the survivors of the Japanese 31st and 15th Divisions passed through in their retreat to Burma. Among the last Japanese strongholds in Manipur, as many as five brigades were directed towards it by the Fourteenth Army in the last phase of the battle. These included the Chindits in the form of the 23rd Long Range Penetration Brigade that sought to cut off

Ukhrul town. Photo by Findlay Kember.

the retreat of the Japanese to the east of Ukhrul. After a week of resistance, the town was recaptured on 8 July.

There is nothing by way of a formal memorial or monument to the Second World War in Ukhrul today. However, the town affords glorious views of the mountains all around, including of the old Point 7378, where a brave defence was attempted in the face of a far larger Japanese force. As you gaze at the surrounding mountains, you appreciate the hardiness of the ordinary Japanese soldier as he made his way through this seemingly insurmountable terrain in March 1944—and through which he made his desperate way back in the pouring rain in July, broken and beaten.

View of Point 7378 (or Harva Khangai) from Ukhrul town.
Photo by Findlay Kember.

Distant view of Jessami from the road to Ukhrul.
Photo by Hemant Singh Katoch.

Kharasom and Jessami

In Manipur, to the far north of Ukhrul, over 100 km away on the border with Nagaland, lies the village of Jessami. It can be accessed from Ukhrul by a narrow winding road that passes through sparsely populated mountains, or by travelling east from Kohima. Both are long journeys on mountain roads and can take around six hours (depending on road conditions). En route from Ukhrul to Jessami is the village of Kharasom. In March 1944 it was at Jessami and Kharasom, together with Shangshak, that the curtain-raiser to the Kohima battle was witnessed.

The 1st Battalion of the Assam Regiment had been deployed to defend these two villages on the approach to Kohima from the east. The regiment had been raised three years earlier and its men came from different parts of Northeast India. At the end of March, they would find themselves in the path of thousands of Japanese soldiers from the 31st Division advancing towards Kohima. They were instructed to fight to the last man.

The Japanese started launching attacks on Kharasom from 27 March, while Jessami began to be targeted from 28 March. For the next four days, assault after assault was directed at the men of the 1st Assam Regiment in the two villages. Sato's units had been ordered to reach Kohima as quickly as possible and the defenders of Kharasom and Jessami stood in their way. The fighting in these two mountain villages was, therefore, fierce and frantic, as both sides strained every sinew to comply with their commands.

The order to fight to the last man was finally withdrawn and the survivors from Jessami withdrew towards Kohima on the night of 1–2 April. Tragically, the news that the order had been rescinded was never received at Kharasom. The company commander there, Captain John M. Young, had nevertheless ordered his remaining men to withdraw. He himself decided to stand his ground, staying with those too seriously wounded to escape. He chose to comply with his existing instruction to fight to the last man and died fighting the Japanese.

Like at Shangshak to the south, the stand at Kharasom and Jessami delayed the Japanese in their advance on Kohima in the crucial opening stage of their offensive. As in 1944, these beautiful mountain villages remain isolated and difficult to get to today. Fortunately, at least an effort has been made to highlight the area's Second World War history: there is a small memorial to the 1st Assam Regiment at a road junction in Jessami. It honours the contribution of the men of this regiment who would go on to fight at Kohima and later in Burma.

Assam Regiment Memorial at Jessami.
Photo by Hemant Singh Katoch.

5. The Mapao–Molvom Range and the Imphal–Kohima Road

'…the tanks of the 2nd Division met the leading infantry of 5th Division at Milestone 109. A convoy, which was waiting for this moment, was at once sent through, and 4 Corps had its first overland supply delivery since the end of March. The Imphal–Kohima battle, the first decisive battle of the Burma campaign, was not yet over, but it was won.'[20]

—Field Marshal Viscount Slim, *Defeat into Victory*

Battle narrative

Besides the Iril River Valley and the Ukhrul Road, Japanese attempts to break through to Imphal from the north in 1944 were focused on the Imphal–Kohima Road (in particular) and the Mapao–Molvom Range. Essentially, Yamauchi's 15th Division targeted the entire arc of mountains that form a sort of semicircle around the northern and north-eastern edges of the Imphal Valley, and tried to use the passages between them to force its way through.

An obvious approach route was the vital Imphal–Kohima–Dimapur Road, the main supply line for 4 Corps. From Imphal the road headed north, climbing upwards to pass over the mountains, crossed Kohima, and then made its descent to Dimapur, the railhead for Manipur. As mentioned earlier, Slim and Scoones had expected the Japanese to target this road, although not with too large a force. But as it turned out, both the Japanese 15th and 31st Divisions made for Imphal, Kohima and the road connecting them.

With regard to Imphal, the cutting of the road near Kangpokpi village by a Japanese raiding unit under the command of the 15th

---

20 Slim, *Defeat into Victory*, p. 397.

Division at the end of March effectively began its siege—albeit the last route into the valley, the much less used Silchar Track, was cut about a fortnight later. Yamauchi's men attempted to reach Imphal via this road, while also making for the higher hill range to the east on which were situated the villages of Mapao and Molvom (or what is referred to in this guide as the Mapao–Molvom Range). East of this range was the Iril River Valley (covered in the previous section).

Facing off with the Japanese in this sector were a range of Fourteenth Army units. For a time, this included the 63rd Indian Brigade (17th Indian Division) after it had withdrawn safely to Imphal; it was later sent back down to the Tiddim Road. But it was left primarily to the men who had been airlifted from the Arakan in Burma to defend Imphal from the north. This initially included two brigades of the 5th Indian Division, which had arrived in the second half of March, as well as one of the 7th Indian Division, which was flown in during early May.

As in the other sectors around Imphal, they first halted the Japanese advance and then turned to the counteroffensive. Through April and May, both the Mapao–Molvom Range and the Imphal–Kohima Road were the focus of their efforts. As the pressure to open the road grew, however, Major General Briggs, commander of the 5th Indian Division, concentrated his forces on the Imphal–Kohima Road north of Imphal through the month of June. It was further felt that opening the road would perhaps more effectively force the Japanese off the heights of the Mapao–Molvom Range as well, instead of the more direct and infinitely harder tactic of battering away at those positions. This would later prove to be an accurate assessment.

The fighting to the north (and immediate north-east) of Imphal was significant in two respects. First, compared to the Japanese 33rd Division battling away on the more distant approach routes to the south, Yamauchi's 15th Division was almost at the gates of Imphal and had the best chance of capturing it. And second, it was finally the opening of the Imphal–Kohima Road on 22 June by the British 2nd Division fighting south from Kohima and the 5th Indian Division battling north from Imphal that marked the defeat of the Japanese offensive in 1944.

Battlefield guide

This guide suggests going up the road from Imphal to Kohima in one day, a journey that can take around six hours, depending on the condition of the road and the number of stops en route. Covering the road in one shot gives you a good feel of it and the terrain alongside; you have the added thrill of knowing that you are travelling on a route taken by many thousands of soldiers during the Second World War.

In relation specifically to the Imphal battle, the following section covers the sites that lie on and around the road between Imphal and Kangpokpi. The battlefields here are the ones connected to the Japanese 15th Division's approach towards Imphal from the north.

The old Imphal Main Airfield (or Koirengei Airfield).
Photo by Hemant Singh Katoch.

The Mapao–Molvom Range as seen from the Imphal–Kohima–Dimapur Road, north of Imphal. Photo by Hemant Singh Katoch.

- Imphal Main

On what are the outskirts of Imphal today is the first stop: the old Imphal Main Airfield, or what is locally known as Koirengei Airfield. This was the most important of all of the airfields that came up in the Imphal Valley during the Second World War. An all-weather strip, it was situated right outside Imphal, running parallel to the Imphal–Kohima Road. At the time of the battle, near it was spread out the 4 Corps headquarters, in an area known as the Keep. This was the nerve centre of the defence of Imphal.

The airfield is no longer in use today. It is under the control of the Indian Army which maintains a fenced-off compound on part of the runway. A line of tall trees separates the airfield from the road today, but these were not there during the war. The best way to access and see the old runway is from either of its northern or southern ends. From here you get a sense of the length and orientation of the airfield, and the hills all around. The skies above Imphal Main today are quiet, a far cry from what it was like in 1944, for Imphal Main was also at the heart of the 'Air Battle of Imphal'. The runway and

Manipur's skies were abuzz with frenetic activity during the battle. In action would have been planes of all kinds: Hurribombers, Spitfires, Vengeance dive bombers and that reliable warhorse, the Dakota, among others.

Reinforcements were flown in in the nick of time, while the injured were flown out for treatment. In fact, the fly-in of the 5th Indian Division from the Arakan to Imphal and Dimapur was the first time an entire infantry division had been airlifted from one battlefield to another. Infantry operations around Imphal and Kohima were supported by bombing and strafing from the air, while Japanese supply lines farther afield were bombarded. Food, ammunition and other provisions were dropped to units that were isolated and cut off. Indeed, 4 Corps at Imphal was able to hold out against the Japanese during the siege precisely because it could rely on the flying in of supplies from the air (known as Operation Stamina). It has been rightly argued that without Allied supremacy and support from the air, the Fourteenth Army would not have won the land battles of Imphal and Kohima. The air effort was spearheaded by squadrons of the 221 Group, Royal Air Force (RAF) and the U.S. Troop Carrier Command.

Imphal Main is also connected to several famed personalities. Arjan Singh, the man who would go on to become an Air Marshal in independent India, commanded an IAF squadron here in 1944. The airfield has a more tragic connection with Major General Orde Wingate, the commander of the Chindits. It was from here that an American B-25 Mitchell bomber took off for Assam on 24 March 1944, with Wingate among its passengers. It would be his last flight: the plane crashed en route in the western hills of Manipur, killing all on board. Finally, it would again be around Imphal Main that Lieutenant General Slim and his three corps commanders would be knighted in December 1944 by Viceroy Wavell.

- Mapao–Molvom Range

There are two ways to view the main peaks of the Mapao–Molvom Range. The first is from the Imphal–Kohima Road itself: in fact, the lower reaches of that range are visible from near Imphal Main. As you continue northwards, from bends in the road you can get distant views of the range, which from Sekmai to present-day Motbung runs roughly parallel to the road (albeit with a lower range of hills in between). You can also go down a country road via Koirengei, get a closer view, and then rejoin the main road near Sekmai, but this can be a bumpy drive. The other way is to approach the range from the east, via the Pangei Road from Imphal. Here you have Nungshigum on one side and the Mapao–Molvom Range on the other. You can keep driving up the road and then follow a smaller road curving left to get a good close-up view.

Whichever route you choose, this is a dramatic battlefield to behold. The range soars above the Imphal Valley, with some of its peaks over 5,000 feet in height. In 1944, the fighting here in particular highlighted the sheer determination of the Japanese soldier at Imphal. By the end of March, the first elements of the 15th Division had already arrived on these heights, posing a real danger to the Keep. Through April it was the men of the 60th Regiment, under the command of Colonel Matsumura, who would come to occupy its heights. From then on, every possible method would be tried, especially by the 5th Indian Division, to try and evict them—but with little success. Although some peaks were eventually recaptured, the Japanese managed to somehow cling on until at least the end of June, long after they had ceased to be in a position to mount new attacks or even to receive any fresh supplies.

Perhaps the peak that best demonstrated this state of affairs was the one the British had named Hump (not to be confused with the nickname for the eastern Himalayas during the Allied airlift to China; see Ledo Road and the Hump section). Attack after attack was launched on the Japanese dug in here. Positioned as they were on the reverse slopes of the feature—a favoured Japanese tactic at Imphal—they seemed impervious to every attack on their positions. The war diaries of the time make for a vivid read. The 3/14th Punjab was tasked with tackling the Japanese on the Hump and the war diaries of their parent 9th Indian Brigade note at least half a dozen attempts to do so through May 1944.

Time and again the infantry would fight its way up, but would be repulsed as soon as it closed in on the top, thanks to showers of grenades and intense machine gun fire, some of which also came from other positions nearby. British artillery and mortar concentrations were directed at the Hump, as were multiple bombing and strafing runs by the air force. But there the Japanese remained on those peaks, come rain (of which there was a lot) or sunshine, determined not to let go. It was a remarkable feat of resistance against all odds.

- Sekmai

As you continue on the road after Imphal Main, the next large settlement you pass is Sekmai, which was a village then. The outskirts of Sekmai were the southernmost limit of the Japanese advance on the road. After taking over Kanglatongbi up the road in the first week of April 1944, Yamauchi's men had put in attacks on Sekmai, but these were beaten off. The last Japanese attack on the Sekmai area had failed by 19 April. It is said that after the failure of this attack, the 15th Division turned largely to the defensive north of Imphal.

Sekmai today is a little town in its own right. The road running through its bazaar is busy with passenger and goods traffic, and the occasional military and paramilitary convoys that are ubiquitous in

Manipur. From the Imphal battle point of view, what is of interest as you travel northwards from Sekmai are both the road you are on and the hills alongside. From April to June 1944, the Japanese had set up roadblocks on the road and dug in on the hills overlooking it, especially east of the road that runs parallel to it. The Imphal turel (river) flows between the road and these hills.

And so, once the Japanese advance had been halted at Sekmai in April, the Fourteenth Army units had the unenviable task of clearing their positions both on and off the road. The subsequent fighting would unfold along two fronts: on the road and in the hills alongside. Each roadblock had to be removed and every threat to movement on the road from positions in the hills had to be eliminated. They had their task cut out for them. Every possible tactic would be employed to achieve their objective: the infantry would mount assaults, the tanks and artillery would provide supporting fire, the air force would be called in to soften the targets. No gains would come easy: as in the other sectors around Imphal, each position regained required equal measures of sheer grit, patience and perseverance.

What makes the drive north beyond Sekmai so special today is that the surroundings still allow you to visualize what it must have been like in 1944. While the villages and towns on the roads have expanded since the time of the war, the hills running alongside even today appear largely unchanged. One of them, called Point 3813, looms into view to the north-east as you cross Sekmai. This had been occupied by the Japanese, but was subsequently recovered in the drive to open the road to the next village, Kanglatongbi, which is also the next stop on the tour.

Distant view of the heights of the Mapao–Molvom Range (in the background) from the east. Photo by Hemant Singh Katoch.

Kanglatongbi War Memorial. Photo by Findlay Kember.

- Kanglatongbi

The Kanglatongbi area was witness to two waves of fighting in 1944. The first was in early April when the Japanese were making their way south. Kanglatongbi was an attractive target: the 221 Advance Ordnance Depot, the largest in Imphal, was located in the area. As the threat from the Japanese increased on the road, some of the most valuable supplies were evacuated southwards to the defensive position at Kanglatongbi known as Lion Box. Manned by a few thousand men, this mainly consisted of administrative and support personnel, with only a smattering of fighting troops. Soon, this was also targeted by the Japanese.

For some four nights, the Japanese continued to attack Lion Box, while the evacuation of supplies continued apace towards Imphal. The men in the box put up a stout defence through it all; during the day they would receive support from infantry and tanks that would move up from Sekmai. As the Japanese assaults intensified, it was decided to withdraw from Lion Box on 7 April, and the Kanglatongbi area was occupied by Yamauchi's 15th Division.

The second phase of fighting took place in subsequent weeks as the British forces battled their way north to open the road. The Japanese had set up roadblocks around Kanglatongbi which had to be tackled one by one. The drive to open the road was stepped up in mid-May and a week later Kanglatongbi had been recovered.

Today Kanglatongbi is home to a dedicated war memorial. The Kanglatongbi War Memorial was inaugurated by the Indian Army Ordnance Corps after the war. It commemorates the battle that was fought there in April 1944 and honours the men of the 221 Advance Ordnance Depot who played a vital role in the area's defence. The memorial is maintained today by the Army Ordnance Corps of the Indian Army.

- Motbung

North of Kanglatongbi lies Motbung. While present-day Motbung is on the road itself, in 1944 it was located in the hills to the east and was referred to as Modbung. This area was the next target in the push to open the road. From early June onwards, this became an entirely 5th Division affair. Its two brigades and their battalions—Indian (mainly) and British—were deployed on both the road and the hills as they battled northwards. Roadblocks were cleared; the infantry pushed ahead, including via hooks around the road; tanks were winched up impossibly steep slopes; and Japanese positions were mortared and shelled.

You can clearly make out the hills around the Modbung position. They are in a line: George, Harry, Isaac and James. The latter two were recaptured by the 2nd Suffolks after an operation from 1 to 9 June. The 3/9th Jats then took up the charge, advancing along the ridgeline east of the road. On the road itself battled forth units such as the 3/14th Punjab and the 2nd West Yorkshires. For a closer look at the hills near the old Modbung position, you can also take a small road heading east out of Motbung town and head towards the Imphal River.

From Motbung the drive up the Imphal–Kohima Road becomes even more atmospheric. The hills close in on both sides of the road, with the Imphal River flowing beside it. You can see how the topography favoured the Japanese and what a challenge it must have been for the British and Indian units to fight their way through. You pass by features with names such as Dot, Dash, Pip, Squeak and Wilfred, and bridges over streams, whose earlier avatars were called London Bridge and Howrah Bridge. So closely clustered are the former that you can barely tell one from the other. By about 13 June, both the road and the hills had been cleared up to the next stop on the road: Saparmeina.

View of the two hill ranges east of the Imphal–Kohima Road. In the foreground are the lower hills with features named Isaac, Harry, James and George. In the background is part of the Mapao-Molvom Range. Photo by Hemant Singh Katoch.

Liver and its vicinity off the Imphal–Kohima Road. The Imphal turel (river) is in the foreground. Photo by Hemant Singh Katoch.

- Saparmeina

It is around Saparmeina village that the final fight was waged to open the road northwards from Imphal in June 1944. It was around here that the 5th Indian Division encountered the final set of Japanese roadblocks and hillside positions, while farther north on the road the British 2nd Division was sweeping south from Kohima. With the monsoon rains in full flow, the conditions were absolutely miserable for all concerned. It rained in bucketloads, turning the hillsides ever more slippery and treacherous. The Imphal River, normally little more than a stream in the dry season, became a raging torrent. There were spells of thick, cold mist, which made the entire area appear dreary and miserable. The military histories of the time paint a truly depressing picture.

If one had to pinpoint a single feature that was most responsible for obstructing the Fourteenth Army's progress around Saparmeina, then it would have to be Liver. The Japanese on this hill simply refused to budge despite being subjected to increasingly powerful attacks by units of the 5th Indian Division. The 3/9th Jats led the infantry attacks and made several attempts up the hill. Artillery concentrations were directed at the Japanese, as were multiple air strikes. But each time the Jat companies fought their way up, they would face intense Japanese fire from Liver and the adjacent hills.

Finally, following a particularly heavy assault on Liver on 21 June involving three Jat companies, the Japanese were found to have slipped away by the next morning. Later that day, the men of the 1/17th Dogras, who had made a wide left hook, met the first units of the British 2nd Division near Milestone 109. Today you can clearly see Liver and the nearby hills around the present-day Saparmeina village from the road itself.

The area near the old Milestone 109. Photo by Findlay Kember.

- Milestone 109

Just over a couple of kilometres after Liver, the road straightens out and the scenery suddenly opens up to the left. The low hills slip away to reveal a beautiful vista of meadows and a much higher mountain range in the distance. It is arguably the prettiest stretch of the road north of Imphal until then and is a welcome change from the more closed-in, curvy drive of the past few kilometres.

This area is also of enormous significance to the twin battles of Imphal and Kohima. For it is on this stretch, near the old Milestone 109 (as measured from Dimapur), that the Fourteenth Army clinched its victory over the Japanese. This is where the men of the British 2nd Division coming south from Kohima and those of the 5th Indian Division fighting up from Imphal met on the morning of 22 June 1944. The road was opened, the siege of Imphal was lifted, and supplies and 33 Corps would soon come flooding in down the road from Kohima. The focus would then shift on clearing the last Japanese strongholds around the Imphal battlefield through the month of July. You can stop off the road in the area today and take a break in a meadow on the left. Further up the road (on the right), a stone marker that highlights the importance of the site has been installed.

Remains of the old bridge on the Imphal–Kohima Road near Kangpokpi that was blown up by the Japanese at the end of March 1944. Photo by Hemant Singh Katoch.

- Kangpokpi bridge

If you do this tour by driving northwards from Imphal, instead of southwards from Kohima, it is the last stop on the road connected to the Imphal battle and which relates most to the battle's commencement. For this is the site of the old bridge over the Imphal River near Kangpokpi, which was blown up by the Japanese at the end of March 1944. The perpetrators belonged to the Honda Raiding Unit (15th Division) that had marched over the mountains from the east against the grain of the country. Its target was to cut the road at Kangpokpi or what was called 'Mission' (there was a Christian Mission near the village at the time). It was this action on the vital land supply route from Dimapur and Kohima that effectively precipitated the siege of Imphal. You can still see the remains of the bridge today to the immediate north of Kangpokpi.

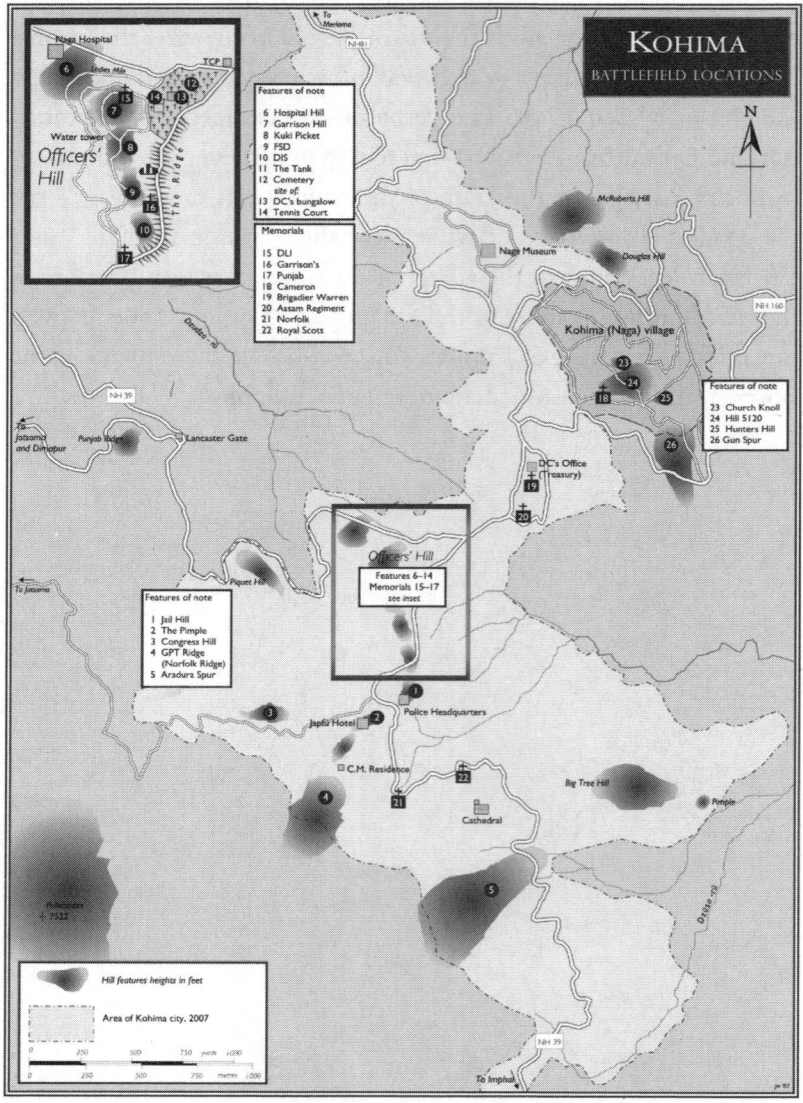

Kohima battlefield locations
Courtesy of the Kohima Educational Society / Kohima Educational Trust.

KOHIMA

'Probably one of the greatest battles in history ... in effect the Battle of Burma ... naked unparalleled heroism ... the British/Indian Thermopylae.'

—Earl Mountbatten

Battle narrative

The main objective of the Japanese offensive in 1944 as authorized by Tokyo was the capture of Imphal. Therefore, it was towards Imphal that the bulk of Mutaguchi's Fifteenth Army was committed. However, his third formation, the 31st Division under the command of Lieutenant General Sato, was tasked with taking a village in the Naga Hills of Assam on the road between Imphal and Dimapur: Kohima. The road looped around the Kohima Ridge as it passed over the mountains that separate the Imphal Valley from the Brahmaputra Valley. For the Japanese, the capture of the Kohima area would block the road and ensure no assistance could be sent down towards Imphal.

As mentioned earlier, Mutaguchi privately harboured ambitions that went beyond the capture of Kohima, something that was anyway not expected to take too long. Dimapur, with its railway line crucial to the American ferrying of supplies to the Chinese via the airfields around Dibrugarh, lay tantalizingly close and made for an even more attractive target. That could potentially pave the way for operations farther afield, together with the involvement of the INA. To him, it all felt eminently doable.

The irony of 1944 was that at least part of this ambition could have been realized. Dimapur could have been taken by the Japanese 31st Division, if only they had tried doing it early enough in the campaign. In fact, Mutaguchi did instruct Sato to do so in April, but this was countermanded by Kawabe. That the fall of Dimapur became a very real possibility was because the British did not anticipate that the Japanese would send such a large force in the direction of Kohima. As already noted, at most the equivalent of a brigade was expected; certainly not an entire division.

This is why it has been argued that while the Fourteenth Army expected a major battle at Imphal and had positioned 4 Corps's formations there accordingly, no such arrangements had been made for Kohima (which also came under Scoones). So, when the Japanese arrived there in early April, the situation was chaotic for the British both in Kohima and in Dimapur. It is also why the siege of Kohima was such a harrowing experience for the defenders of the ill-prepared garrison as some 1,500 men suddenly found themselves facing a Japanese force of some 15,000.

The most famous of the defenders of Kohima were the 4th Royal West Kents, part of the 161st Indian Brigade (5th Indian Division) that had been flown in to Dimapur from the Arakan. But the garrison included men from several other units as well—including the 1st Assam Regiment, the 3rd Assam Rifles, the 3/2nd Punjab—who fought hard at Kohima. These were brought under the command of 33 Corps, which took charge of the area once it became clear that Scoones would have his hands full in dealing with the situation around Imphal. Lieutenant General Stopford was the corps commander.

As the first Japanese arrived in the Kohima area, the garrison scrambled to get its defences in order. The movement of the West Kents up the road to Kohima typified the chaos reigning at the time and the confusion about where the main Japanese blow was going to fall—Kohima or Dimapur. At the end of March, they had been rushed up to Kohima. Just as they were digging in, they were suddenly instructed by Stopford to move down the road towards Dimapur. Despite howls of protests by the other commanders at Kohima, who maintained that Kohima would be the main target (and not Dimapur), the West Kents moved out. But this decision had to be reversed just days later and the West Kents were sent back up to Kohima even as the first Japanese had already arrived.

In the popular imagination, the West Kents symbolize the siege of April 1944 that followed, the phase of the fighting at Kohima for which it is best known today. That was when the beleaguered Kohima garrison defended an ever-shrinking part of the Kohima Ridge against wave after wave of Japanese attacks. Outnumbered ten to one, and cut off on all sides, they held out for about a fortnight, before they were relieved by reinforcements coming up the road from Dimapur, mainly in the form of the British 2nd Division.

A longer battle until June 1944 followed the siege, with the Japanese proving next to impossible to dislodge from Kohima and its surrounding heights. It was fighting of the most vicious kind between the two sides, often at close quarters, in towering, jungle-covered mountains. The British forces involved included their 2nd Division, under the command of Major General Grover. This division consisted of a line-up from some of the most renowned regiments of the British Army (see Orders of Battle). They would soon be joined by two brigades of the 7th Indian Division which was flown in from the Arakan to Dimapur.

The initial British strategy during this second phase of the battle was to launch a three-pronged attack on the Japanese positions in the Kohima area. For Major General Grover, this involved sending his three brigades in moves to the left, centre and right. On the left, the 5th Brigade was sent from the main road around Zubza to the Merema Ridge, having to cross the ravine of a nullah en route. It was to then move towards Naga Village. The 6th Brigade was directed to the main positions of the Kohima Ridge at the centre; it was soon joined by the 33rd Indian Brigade (7th Indian Division). The 4th Brigade was sent on a wide flanking march to the right. It was to climb the imposing mountains in between and arrive on the road to Imphal below the Aradura Spur.

In the final stage of the battle, after the recovery of the ridge, the British strategy focused on the two remaining strongholds of the Japanese at Kohima: Naga Village and Aradura Spur. The 7th Indian Division was told to tackle the Naga Village area on the left, while the British 2nd Division was given responsibility for the Aradura Spur area to the right. These last few days of fighting, until the beginning of June, also proved difficult and stretched both sides to the limits of their endurance.

What dogged the Japanese throughout the Kohima battle was inadequate supplies. After their initial rations had finished, the men of the 31st Division received no supplies over the mountains they had rapidly crossed at the start of the offensive. Like at Imphal, the Fourteenth Army's units did not crumble at their arrival—and left no provisions to be easily acquired. Once Kohima did not fall in the first fortnight of the battle when the attackers far outnumbered the defenders, its conclusion was foregone. With the arrival of British and Indian reinforcements and without supplies, the Japanese could only hang on for so long. What is remarkable is just how long Sato's men were able to hold out in the face of impossible odds—it was only in early June 1944 that they started withdrawing from the bloodied battlefields of Kohima.

A panorama of Kohima from the Kohima Cathedral area (the old Aradura Spur). Below the tree line near the top-left is the old GPT Ridge, and behind it, the TV tower area, is Jotsoma. The big building of the Nagaland Police Headquarters (centre-right) is on the old Jail Hill; the tree covered area to its right is the Kohima Ridge; and the concentration of buildings on the extreme right is the old Naga Village. Photo by Hemant Singh Katoch.

Battlefield guide

The thing to remember is that while in Manipur it was a battle *for* Imphal, here it truly was a battle *of* Kohima. Britons, Indians, Gurkhas and Japanese literally fought for almost every square inch of Kohima in 1944, unlike in the south with its fighting on and around the different spokes leading to the hub at Imphal. The Kohima battlefield, then, is actually a very small, compact area compared to the spread-out and widely dispersed battlefields of Imphal.

The other point to note is that the Kohima of 1944 was very different from the city that it has become today. All accounts of the battle highlight that the area was sparsely populated, with large parts of it covered in jungle. But Kohima has grown enormously since then and is today the busy capital of Nagaland. As a result, many of the old battlefields and hillsides are covered in a jungle of another kind: concrete buildings. This usually comes as a bit of a surprise to any visitor whose only points of reference about Kohima are historical accounts and their black-and-white photos dating back to 1944. It also jolts those who have come up from Imphal where battlefields like Nungshigum, Scraggy, Gibraltar and the Hump seem to have changed little since the time of the war.

Having said that, and once you adjust to the new reality of how built up Kohima is today, you soon realize that there is still much to look out for and appreciate in terms of its Second World War past. For one, as you gaze upon Kohima from one of the vantage points around town, you are immediately struck by the topography. Already at an altitude of almost 5,000 feet, the town is surrounded by even higher mountains. Fortunately, the upper reaches of some of them are still covered in thick forest, giving one a sense of what it must have been like during the war. You immediately understand the basic fact about the impossible terrain the battle was fought in. And you can only truly comprehend this when you see Kohima for yourself.

Before exploring the Kohima area, one needs to orient oneself as to its general layout. The famed Kohima Ridge is the ridge to which the road from Imphal comes up from the south, curls around, and then descends towards Dimapur. This is the epicentre of the 1944 battle, its peaks making up the most iconic battlefields of the time. Across from it, roughly to the north-east, lies the original Kohima village, which is referred to as Naga Village in war accounts. Northwest of Kohima village and down the ridgeline there lies Merema. To the south of the Kohima Ridge and overlooking the entire area are the Aradura Spur and its neighbouring General Purpose Transport (GPT) Ridge (a war-era name) and Mount Puliebadze (or Pulie Badze). Above the road to Dimapur, a couple of miles down from Kohima, is Jotsoma village; further down the road is Zubza. These places make up, more or less, the main canvas against which the 1944 battle was fought, with the Kohima Ridge, the Naga Village of that time and the Aradura Spur area arguably forming its core battlefields.

As you set about exploring Kohima, the final thing to bear in mind is this: vantage points. To really understand the battle, you must try and go to as many of the accessible vantage points in and around Kohima as possible. For it is then, when you look at the battlefield from different angles, altitudes and perspectives, zooming in and out of the main locations, that you can grasp the nuances of the battle and the perspectives of the warring sides.

IMPHAL–KOHIMA, 1944

View of the Kohima Ridge from the old Naga Village. In the centre is the tree-covered old Garrison Hill; the Kohima War Cemetery, where the old district commissioner's bungalow was in 1944; and part of the old Kuki Piquet, with the water tower on its extreme left.
Photo by Findlay Kember.

A view of the Kohima Ridge on the right (under the shade) and the old Naga Village (Kohima Village) straight ahead, from the direction of Jotsoma. The Imphal–Kohima–Dimapur Road can be seen looping around the ridge; the old IGH Spur can be seen just above the curve on the road on the left. Photo by Findlay Kember.

1. Kohima Ridge

If there was a fulcrum of this Second World War battle, it was the Kohima Ridge. It was around this ridge that the road from Imphal to Dimapur looped, and its possession was key to control over movements on the road. In 1944, atop the Kohima Ridge were a number of civilian and army installations the British had built over time. They were spread out over a series of heights, which were referred to in the battle as Garrison Hill (or Summerhouse Hill), Kuki Piquet, Field Supply Depot (FSD) and Detail Issue Store (DIS). On the slope of Garrison Hill that stretched to the northeast towards a road junction lay the district commissioner's (DC) bungalow, with the famed tennis court behind it. On another spur extending north-west was a hospital; this was known as IGH (Indian General Hospital) Spur or Hospital Spur. To the immediate south of DIS and across the Imphal–Dimapur road lay Jail Hill, so named after the local jail at its base.

This was the concentrated area that was witness to some of the bitterest combat seen anywhere during the Second World War. As mentioned earlier, there were two distinct phases of fighting in 1944, and the Kohima Ridge was at the heart of both. The first phase lasted from about 4 to 20 April, and this has become famous as the Kohima Siege. This was when the Japanese 31st Division surrounded the garrison and tried their level best to capture its last redoubts on the Kohima Ridge. The British positions fell one by one as the Japanese launched wave upon wave of attacks. Although the latter were able to capture most of the ridge, they were unable to overrun the garrison in the face of a heroic defence.

So began the second phase of the fighting on the ridge, which lasted until around mid-May. This involved the effort by those who relieved the siege to try and recover its heights from the Japanese. It was to be another bitter struggle. Once the ridge had been retaken, the focus of the fighting shifted towards evicting Sato's men from their other strongholds around Kohima (Naga Village, Aradura Spur).

The best way to explore the old Kohima Ridge is on foot. You can drive part of the way too, but you risk either getting stuck in the city's notorious traffic or driving by without understanding what you are seeing. The area is very built up today and it is only during a walk that you can take it all in and appreciate the different positions that made up the old Kohima Ridge in 1944. This guide suggests a walk lasting a couple of hours in a loop, starting from and ending at the Kohima War Cemetery.

It is tempting to get started with the cemetery itself. But it is, arguably, more interesting to walk the main battlefield first and then look around the cemetery at leisure. To begin the walk, exit the cemetery's car park, cross the main road from Imphal and turn right, that is, heading southwards as per the compass, but up the slope as far as the road is concerned. From here on you should keep walking along the main road for just short of a kilometre, until you reach an intersection where there is a right turn. You should cross the road again and take that turn. In the kilometre or so you cover this way, you are essentially walking along the main Imphal–Kohima–Dimapur Road, under one side of the old ridge. It is now that the positions one has read about start to make sense.

- Garrison Hill–Jail Hill

The car park and the cemetery are laid out on the lower reaches of Garrison Hill. But today, the cemetery area is a separate hill by itself. The reason being that a short road has been carved right through a part of the old Garrison Hill, which connects to the road to Dimapur on the other side of the cemetery. This has probably been done to lessen the pressure of traffic at the main Traffic Control Point (TCP) a short distance away, but it is disconcerting the first time to realize that the old Garrison Hill has been split into two.

As you continue on, you walk by the main Garrison Hill, atop which today lies Raj Bhavan, the official residence of the Governor of Nagaland. One thing that immediately strikes you from the road is the steepness of the hills, up and down which both sides launched multiple attacks and counterattacks during the battle. The other point is just how compact the entire area is. Considering that the fighting raged on the Kohima Ridge through April and until about mid-May, this is a fairly small area to pack in a fight of this duration involving a few thousand men.

The Imphal–Kohima–Dimapur Road as it curves around the old Kuki Piquet on the Kohima Ridge.
Photo by Hemant Singh Katoch.

The tank at Kohima. Photo by Findlay Kember.

Next up you can make out the shape of the old Kuki Piquet, after which comes the larger FSD and then the old DIS, around which the road curves and leads to the traffic intersection with the right turn. Kuki Piquet can also be spotted from around Kohima by the water tower on it.

It is along the road at the base of the old Kuki Piquet (to your right) and FSD (to your left) that you find a remarkable reminder of the Second World War: a tank. Amazingly, this Lee/Grant of the 3rd Carabiniers lies today exactly where it fell during the battle in 1944. An enclosure has since been built around it and there are helpful plaques and markers that explain its history. The tank had been involved in supporting the British 2nd Division's operations on the ridge in May. On the sixth of that month, it had careered down the slope in heavy rain and crashed against a tree. Coming under Japanese fire, the crew jammed its machine guns to fire continuously, set the tank's turret to rotate, and escaped. It remains, undisturbed, as a memorial to the battle.

Garrison Memorial. Photo by Hemant Singh Katoch.

Part of the old DIS, with the Imphal–Kohima–Dimapur Road running around it. The Punjab Memorial is also visible to the left.
Photo by Hemant Singh Katoch.

Continuing on the road, walking past the old positions of FSD and DIS, there is a major curve in the road, which leads to a traffic intersection. The hill on the left, along which the main road continues, is the old Jail Hill. It is covered with buildings today, the grandest of which houses the headquarters of the Nagaland Police on top of the hill, which allows you to easily spot the feature from miles around. You cross the road at the small intersection and take the right turn. There, on the corner of this hillside (the old DIS), lies the Punjab memorial. This is dedicated to the men of the 4/15th Punjab Regiment who had fought and died on this hill (DIS) in May 1944. Also inscribed are the names of the fallen from the 4/1st Gurkha Rifles, its sister battalion in the 33rd Indian Brigade, and those of the Punjabis who were killed in the subsequent fighting in Naga Village. This brigade was part of the 7th Indian Division which had been flown in from Burma and whose men played an integral role in the recapture of the Kohima area from the Japanese.

Punjab Memorial. Photo by Hemant Singh Katoch.

Assam Rifles Memorial. Photo by Hemant Singh Katoch.

Spotting and visiting as many of these war memorials as possible is a key feature of a Kohima battlefield tour. Many of the regimental and other memorials that were once to be found scattered across Kohima have since been relocated to the war cemetery. This is a natural consequence of the growth and urbanization of the area since the Second World War, with the memorials increasingly finding themselves hemmed in by buildings and development. Some, such as the Punjab memorial, however, have thankfully still survived in their original locations and serving to remind us that these very hills were the old battlefields of 1944.

- Assam Rifles Memorial–Garrison Hill

After the traffic and noise of the main road to Imphal, this stretch of the walk on the old Kohima Ridge is a welcome change. Vehicles are fewer, the area quieter. This is because even today it is where several official buildings and residences are located. You should follow the road which forks to the right and leads to The Heritage and Raj Bhavan. Near the fork is an Assam Rifles memorial (called 'Dhai Murty'), which marks the assistance they provided to refugees from Burma in 1942.

One is now essentially walking the most fought over ground at Kohima: the ridge itself. As the Japanese arrived at Kohima in early April, they attacked the ridge from two main directions. The first was from the south, from the direction of the road to Imphal; the second was from the north-east, from the direction of Naga Village. With regard to the former, they positioned themselves on the heights south of the ridge, including the Aradura Spur. They then pushed on. One by one, the positions fell to the Japanese. Among the first to go was GPT Ridge. You can see this ridge to the south—it is distinguished by a series of orderly looking buildings that protrude like a triangle into the woods. An Indian flag sits on the northern end of this built-up area, above which the treeline begins (see the Aradura Spur section for more).

After GPT Ridge, the Japanese forced the evacuation of Jail Hill on 6 April. The next target was DIS, the southernmost feature on the ridge. This is where the Punjab memorial lies today. From the memorial onwards, the cluster of buildings to the right are also on the old DIS. Like the other hills of the ridge, it was witness to two phases of intense fighting in 1944: the Japanese advance in the siege and then again the British and Indian counterattack that followed. Interestingly, DIS is associated with one of the most famous personalities of the Kohima battle: Lance Corporal John Harman of the Royal West Kents.

It was for his actions on and around DIS on 8–9 April that Harman was posthumously awarded the Victoria Cross. This is when he single-handedly, and in the face of intense Japanese fire, destroyed a machine gun position and then attacked another post, killing its occupants. Harman was finally killed by machine gun fire when he was walking back to British lines; he is said to have died in the arms of his company commander.

You now follow the road going up the slope of the next feature on the ridge: FSD. After the British evacuated DIS on 10th April, this became their frontline position in the south. Today The Heritage hotel stands on top of FSD. This was the then district commissioner's new bungalow that was constructed after his previous one was destroyed in the battle; it is today an atmospheric heritage hotel perfect for a brief halt. Adjacent to it is the old Kuki Piquet, distinguishable by the water tower on it. After a week of heavy fighting, the Japanese were able to press forward and capture both these positions on the night of 17th April. The Kohima Ridge was nearly lost: all that was left to be taken by Sato's men was Garrison Hill, including one side of the tennis court and part of IGH Spur.

As you continue the walk, you see before you the peak of the old Garrison Hill, which is today Nagaland's Raj Bhavan. The area is under tight security and you should take a left in front of the main gate, follow the road for about a hundred yards, and take the small staircase going down. This will bring you to a quiet road that then loops around Garrison Hill. Below the road, but not visible from it, is the old IGH Spur; it is now where the present-day Naga Hospital is located. It is when you are walking this old battlefield that you realize just how close the British had come to losing Kohima in 1944. By the end of the siege the garrison had been packed into an area that was just a few hundred yards in length and width.

The conditions in which the fighting had raged on the ridge had been simply appalling. As if the treacherous terrain was not difficult enough, the defenders of the Kohima garrison had to endure night after night of increasingly frenzied attacks by the Japanese. Infantry charges, grenade attacks, mortaring, shelling by field and mountain guns, sniper fire—everything was directed at those besieged men who, with each passing day, were losing hope of ever being relieved. It is said that the stench of death hung in the air on the ridge as the bodies of men of both sides lay decomposing in the open. Things were especially bad in the hospital area where, at times, injured men who lay on stretchers were at the receiving end of yet more Japanese fire; if they had somehow survived until then, the latter then finished some of them off. It is nothing short of a miracle that the Kohima Ridge did not fall in April 1944.

As the road curves around the hill, one should look out for vantage points in the area. From here you can see several places that are key to understanding the Kohima battle. Towards the right is the old Naga Village (or main Kohima town today), one of the main strongholds of the Japanese and from where they had launched attacks on the northern parts of the ridge. Roughly in the centre stretches out the Merema Ridge, on which the Japanese were also present; it was along this ridge that the 5th Brigade had later advanced towards Naga Village. And finally, to the left are visible parts of two villages that played a crucial role in 1944. The first is Jotsoma, which can be easily identified by the massive television tower in it, and the second is Zubza in the far distance on the road to Dimapur.

During the siege, the Japanese had cut off the Kohima Ridge from Jotsoma, where the remaining units of the 161st Indian Brigade were. The latter, in turn, had been cut off from Zubza further south—the Japanese had blocked the road in between. Zubza was where the first units of the British 2nd Division had arrived as they pushed on towards Kohima from Dimapur. From both these villages protective artillery fire had been directed at the Kohima area.

Looking north towards Merema Ridge from a rooftop on the old Garrison Hill. Photo by Hemant Singh Katoch.

The terraces of the Kohima War Cemetery, with a view of the old Naga Village (Kohima Village) spread out on the hill across.
Photo by Hemant Singh Katoch.

2. Kohima War Cemetery

Back on the road again, you then descend a staircase to the main road and walk down a couple of hundred yards back to where you started from. Having walked the main battlefields of the ridge, it is time to explore what is arguably one of the most spectacular war cemeteries in the world: the Kohima War Cemetery. Several aspects make it an exceptional site. For one, the cemetery itself is on an old battlefield—it bore the brunt of the Japanese attacks on the ridge that came from the direction of Naga Village. The cemetery also encompasses the site where the DC's Bungalow was in 1944, which saw heavy fighting both during and after the siege.

Second, it is laid out in a series of beautiful terraces up the hillside, with terrific views to be had of the Kohima area. On the terraces are laid out in neat rows over 1,400 graves of Commonwealth soldiers who died in and around Kohima during the Second World War. On the highest point of the cemetery is the Cremation Memorial which commemorates over 900 Hindu and Sikh soldiers who were killed.

British 2nd Division Memorial at the Kohima War Cemetery. It bears the immortal words of the Kohima Epitaph. Photo by Findlay Kember.

Outline of the old tennis court, Kohima War Cemetery. Photo by Findlay Kember

Third, within the cemetery's compound lies what is surely among the unlikeliest of Second World War battlefields in the world. This is the tennis court behind the old DC's Bungalow, the outline of which the CWGC has marked and maintained to this day. On one side of the court had been men of the Japanese Fifteenth Army and on the other side had been those of the British Fourteenth Army. Attack after attack had been launched across this very tennis court during the battle. Remarkably, after several unsuccessful attempts, the

British managed to bring armour on the tennis court and the area of the DC's Bungalow to assist the infantry in evicting the Japanese from the area. This tactic worked, with the tanks firing on the Japanese positions at point-blank range. The Cross of Sacrifice is also to be found today on part of the tennis court.

But perhaps what makes the cemetery and indeed this battle famous the world over are the immortal words of the Kohima Epitaph. These are inscribed on the memorial dedicated to the British 2nd Division, one of several memorials to be found at the cemetery. The epitaph is still invoked, not just of the battle at Kohima or Imphal, but often in remembrance of the entire Burma Campaign. Its words continue to resonate among people today:

'When you go home, tell them of us and say,

For your tomorrow, we gave our today.'

Cremation Memorial, Kohima War Cemetery. Photo by Findlay Kember.

View of the old Aradura Spur in the far distance from the Kohima War Cemetery. Photo by Hemant Singh Katoch.

3. Aradura Spur and GPT Ridge

From the cemetery and the ridge, the Kohima Cathedral is the next site one can visit. The massive structure is built on the lower reaches of what was called the Aradura Spur. Today the upper reaches of the Aradura Spur remain largely uninhabited, while the lower reaches are covered with buildings. From the grounds of the cathedral and especially the road just above it, you get a different view of the battlefield: from the south. You see it from a Japanese perspective, for the Aradura Spur was a major stronghold of the Japanese during the battle, from where they targeted the Kohima Ridge from the south. These were also parts from where the Japanese proved especially difficult to evict; indeed, the Aradura Spur area was where Sato's men held out right until the end of the battle.

Japanese veterans and family members of some of the men who died in 1944 contributed to the construction of the Kohima Cathedral. Near the back gate of the compound there is a plaque in English and Japanese that notes the connection with the battle. Its moving inscription includes the following words:

> 'If the people of Kohima, along with priests, keep the thoughts of the dead soldiers in their hearts for all the long years to come, and pray for the peace and prosperity they desired, there could be no better prayer for the souls of the departed.'

Distant view of Kohima Cathedral on the lower reaches of the old Aradura Spur. Photo by Findlay Kember.

Kohima Cathedral. Photo by Findlay Kember.

The plaque behind the Kohima Cathedral. Photo by Findlay Kember.

From the cathedral area you get excellent views of not just the ridge and the old Naga Village, but also of what were Jail Hill and GPT Ridge. As mentioned earlier, the former can be identified thanks to the large blue-roofed white building of the Nagaland Police headquarters, while the latter can be marked by the buildings just below the treeline. These two features were the first to be lost to the Japanese as they approached Kohima from the south in early April 1944. Once in their possession, Sato's men dug in and built up formidable defensive positions. They created a network of bunkers, tunnels and trenches in the hills; defensive positions were often interlocking, making them almost impenetrable.

This is why it later proved so difficult to evict them from both Jail Hill and GPT Ridge. In fact, the operations to recover the two were interlinked: the men fighting to recapture Jail Hill had to contend with intense Japanese fire raining on them from the GPT Ridge area. This was to be a consistent problem at Kohima where almost every position was either overlooked by or was in the direct line of sight of another. It was the same with GPT Ridge and Jail Hill where the Japanese on the former had to be neutralized before the latter could be taken. This was learnt the hard way as at least one attack on Jail Hill ended in mass casualties because of the Japanese bunkers on GPT Ridge.

The fight to recapture GPT Ridge was led by the 4th Brigade and its battalion of the Royal Norfolks in particular. The brigade had been sent on a flanking march behind the mountains and, in a revised instruction, told to take the GPT Ridge area. It was no easy task. While some of the Japanese bunkers on the upper reaches were captured, those on the lower reaches took a lot longer to subdue. It was for his actions in this operation on GPT Ridge that a Victoria Cross was posthumously awarded to Captain John Niel Randle of the Royal Norfolks (see box). By mid-May the recapture of both

GPT Ridge (by 4th Brigade) and Jail Hill (by 33rd Indian Brigade) was complete.

View of the GPT Ridge area from the Kohima Cathedral (old Aradura Spur). Photo by Hemant Singh Katoch.

View of the Nagaland Police Headquarters on the old Jail Hill and parts of the Kohima Ridge (covered in trees). Photo by Hemant Singh Katoch.

VC Citation for Captain John Niel Randle

On the 4th May, 1944, at Kohima in Assam, a Battalion of the Norfolk Regiment attacked the Japanese positions on a nearby ridge. Captain Randle took over command of the Company which was leading the attack, when the Company Commander was severely wounded. His handling of a difficult situation in the face of heavy fire was masterly and although wounded himself in the knee by grenade splinters he continued to inspire his men by his initiative, courage and outstanding leadership, until the Company had captured its objective and consolidated its position. He then went forward and brought in all the wounded men lying outside the perimeter.

In spite of his painful wound Captain Randle refused to be evacuated and insisted on carrying out a personal reconnaissance with great daring in bright moonlight prior to a further attack by his Company on the positions to which the enemy had withdrawn.

At dawn on 6th May the attack opened led by Captain Randle and one of the platoons succeeded in reaching the crest of the hill held by the Japanese. Another platoon, however, ran into heavy medium machine gun fire from a bunker on the reverse slope of the feature. Captain Randle immediately appreciated that this particular bunker covered not only the rear of his new position but also the line of communication of the Battalion and, therefore, the destruction of the enemy post was imperative if the operation was to succeed.

With utter disregard of the obvious danger to himself Captain Randle charged the Japanese machine gun post single-handed with rifle and bayonet. Although bleeding in the face and mortally wounded by numerous bursts of machine gun fire he reached the bunker and silenced the gun with a grenade thrown through the bunker slit. He then flung his body across the slit so that the aperture should be completely sealed.

The bravery shown by this officer could not have been surpassed and by his self-sacrifice he saved the lives of many of

> his men and enabled not only his own Company but the whole Battalion to gain its objective and win a decisive victory over the enemy.[21]

Memorial to the Royal Norfolk Regiment. Photo by Hemant Singh Katoch.

Memorial to the Royal Scots. Photo by Findlay Kember.

---

21 Supplement to the *London Gazette*, 12 December 1944.

As mentioned earlier, the Aradura Spur was the last Japanese stronghold to hold out at Kohima. The battle in the area, waged by the units of British 2nd Division (the Norfolks and Royal Scots in particular), involved campaigning at its hardest. It was also enormously frustrating and disheartening for the men, who had been in the jungle hills of Kohima in pouring rain for weeks on end. The Japanese here were ultimately forced to withdraw south once they found themselves outflanked by British troops coming in from the east.

Memorials to the Assam Rifles and the Assam Regiment.
Photo by Hemant Singh Katoch.

Memorial to Brigadier (later Major General) Warren.
Photo by Hemant Singh Katoch.

Today, far below the cathedral and along the main road to Imphal, lie two British memorials. There is the Royal Scots memorial, which is on a hillside, and the Norfolks memorial, which is just off the road in its own little compound. These memorials are easy to miss amidst the surrounding buildings, and the traffic and noise of the main road and bazaar. And yet, there they are, amidst all the construction and bustle of a present-day city, reminding us of the historic events of 1944.

4. Naga Village

Having visited the main spots on the ridge and south of it in town, one should also take time out to visit areas farther north. The obvious one is the old Naga Village (present-day Kohima village). This takes you through the main bazaar area, which is usually busy, and where the traffic moves slowly. En route, you can make a quick detour to the office of the District Commissioner on what used to be the Treasury Hill. There, along the road, is a memorial to Brigadier Warren, the commander of the 161st Indian Brigade. He died in a plane crash while flying from Burma to Assam in early February 1945. Another memorial to see, closer to the TCP, is that of the Assam Regiment, which is in a small enclosure off the main road, together with one dedicated to the Assam Rifles.

Continuing on, the next stop is a viewing or observation tower that has been erected on the highest point of the old Naga Village. Although it seems to have been installed for the viewing pleasure of the local residents and possibly tourists, it actually serves the purpose of anyone visiting the battlefield exceedingly well. From its highest point you see spread before you, in a 360-degree panorama—barring the occasional mobile telephone tower—all of Kohima and the surrounding areas. On a clear day, the view on offer is the best that can be possibly had of the entire battlefield. From there you can easily chart the course of the events of 1944, from the siege to the battle that followed, and where both armies and their formations were. A visit to Kohima is incomplete without visiting this spot.

As one takes in the scene, one is also reminded of the actions of a less talked about military formation that played an active role in Kohima. And that is of the 23rd Long Range Penetration Brigade (the Chindits). While most of the Chindit formations were in action behind Japanese lines in Burma at this time, this brigade had been sent to assist the Kohima battle. But they did not directly participate in the fighting; their main task was to harass the Japanese in the rear areas and, later in the battle, to disrupt and hinder their retreat. They did so effectively, including at Ukhrul, all the while marching and navigating through miles of treacherous country.

As it so happens, the observation tower you are standing on is on a battlefield itself. Not only is it a part of the much fought over old Naga Village, but it is around its highest point, known during the battle as Hill 5120. Another Japanese stronghold at the time, this area and the nearby features of Hunters Hill and Gun Spur were, like the Aradura Spur, some of the last to be retaken by the Fourteenth Army at Kohima. The British counterattacks here were launched along the Merema Ridge and, once the main Kohima Ridge was recovered, from the south as well. The entire area was finally recaptured at the beginning of June. This allowed Major General Grover to send a column (5th Brigade) from the old Assam Barracks area nearby (the Assam Rifles compound today) on a left hook and outflank the Japanese on Aradura Spur.

View of parts of Kohima Ridge (centre-left) and the surrounding mountains from the old Naga Village (Kohima Village).

Memorial to the Queen's Own Cameron Highlanders, Kohima. Photo by Findlay Kember.

Panorama showing the route of the left hook by 5th Brigade to outflank the Japanese on Aradura Spur in June 1944. Seen here are parts of the old Assam Barracks (left) and the hills en route named Dyer Hill, Pimple and Big Tree Hill. Photo by Hemant Singh Katoch.

There are two reminders of the battle in the old Naga Village area today. The first is a memorial at the base of the tower. This is dedicated to the men of the 1st Queen's Own Cameron Highlanders who fought here. The second is a small private museum nearby, which showcases a private collection of relics and remnants of war.

5. Merema Ridge

From the old Naga Village you can continue on towards Merema. It was from here, along the Merema Ridge, that the main push against the Japanese in the village had come. From the Merema area you get an excellent view of the main road to Dimapur and parts of the villages of Jotsoma and Zubza. You can clearly see how the British forces had been placed during the siege on and around the road: the garrison at Kohima, cut off from the rest of the 161st Indian Brigade at Jotsoma which, in turn, was cut off from the British 2nd Division at Zubza. In between lies the deep nullah which units of the 5th Brigade had to discreetly cross to get over to this side.

6. Kisama, Kigwema and the Road to Imphal

A Second-World-War-era Bailey Bridge south of Kohima on the Imphal–Kohima–Dimapur Road. Photo by Findlay Kember.

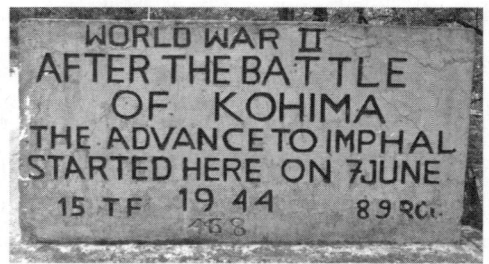

Stone marker near Kohima on the Imphal–Kohima–Dimapur Road. Photo by Findlay Kember.

The Imphal part of this guide covered the Imphal–Kohima Road only up to Kangpokpi. But the drive between the two cities is an incredibly scenic one and is well worth the effort. You also cross en route several sites connected to the twin battles of 1944. There are the places where the Japanese rearguard retreating from Kohima tried to slow the advance of the British 2nd Division, including at Viswema in Nagaland and Maram in Manipur. A road marker indicating the spot where the 2nd Division started their march southwards from Kohima towards Imphal in June 1944 can be seen alongside the road. Finally, an old, abandoned Bailey Bridge can be found near the village of Khuzama, while another survives just near Chumukedima (short of Dimapur).

Diorama depicting fighting on the tennis court at the World War II Museum in Kisama. Photo by Findlay Kember.

World War II Museum in Kisama. Photo by Findlay Kember.

- World War II Museum, Kisama

There is an excellent museum dedicated to the Kohima battle in Kisama, to the south of Kohima. It is located in the Naga Heritage Village, the same complex which is home to the famous Hornbill Festival that takes place in December every year. The museum contains relics of war, dioramas and excellent information panels and displays on the battle, including about the main armies and personalities involved. You can visit the museum either when you are driving up the road from Imphal to Kohima (it is just off the road) or vice versa. A separate visit to the museum can also be made from Kohima. In non-Hornbill Festival times the museum is usually open for some three hours every weekday, so any visit has to be carefully planned.

- Kigwema

Kigwema lies to the south of Kisama. In recent times there has been some interest in the village as locals claim that this is where Sato had stayed during the battle (visitors are even shown a specific house). Another building in the village has the following words painted on one of its walls: 'Japanese troops arrived at Kigwema on 4-4-44 at 3 p.m. during World War II.'

Memorial in Jotsoma that honours Major General John M.L. Grover.
Photo by Findlay Kember.

Local memorial to the fallen at Gagiphe, near Jotsoma.
Photo by Hemant Singh Katoch.

7. Jotsoma

To the west of Kohima lies Jotsoma. This village is closely linked to the entire Kohima battle. The bulk of the 161st Indian Brigade was in Jotsoma during the siege in April 1944. The Japanese had cut the road between Dimapur and Kohima both ahead and behind Jotsoma (the road ran below the village). As noted earlier, it was from near Jotsoma that the artillery was able to provide absolutely critical fire in support of the garrison throughout the siege. Expertly guided by the commander of the only artillery battery at Kohima at the time, thousands of rounds were fired from this mountain village in what is seen as a decisive contribution to British victory. After the siege, and once the road to Kohima was open, Jotsoma became the base of Major General Grover of the British 2nd Division.

Today there is much to see around Jotsoma connected to the 1944 battle. The most striking structure is the memorial constructed by the villagers to honour Major General Grover. The Grover Memorial was unveiled in a colourful ceremony during the 70th anniversary commemoration of the Kohima battle in April 2014 when the entire village turned up for the occasion. It is located at the site said to be that of Major General Grover's headquarters.

Also worth exploring in the heights around Jotsoma are a couple of smaller memorials built by the Nagas in remembrance of the battle. Both of these involve climbs up steep slopes and it is strongly recommended that these are attempted with the help of a local guide. The memorial at Gagiphe peak is dedicated to soldiers of both sides, while the one closer to the village honours the Japanese soldiers who fell at Kohima. Remains of trenches and bunkers can still be found on the trek up to Gagiphe. This trek follows a route roughly parallel to the much more popular one up to Puliebadze (or Pulie Badze), the peak which overlooks Kohima and has a large cross atop it. From here, too, you get stunning views of the city.

If you go to Jotsoma, it is well worth driving another half an hour—albeit a bumpy road—to Khonoma. A walk through this beautiful village, billed as the country's first 'green village', gives you a glimpse of the traditional way of life of the Nagas. This was also the route taken by the 4th Brigade in its wide flanking march around Kohima.

Local memorial near Jotsoma honouring the Japanese soldiers who lost their lives at Kohima in 1944. Photo by Hemant Singh Katoch.

Marker that mentions Bunker Hill near Zubza where the Japanese had set up a road block in April 1944.

8. Zubza

On the drive from Kohima to Dimapur, you cross the village of Zubza. From the bends in the road here you get the last view of the Kohima Ridge as you descend towards Dimapur—or the first, if you are coming up the other way. It was near here, astride the road at the old Milestone 37½, that the Japanese had set up a roadblock during the siege in April 1944. Units of the British 2nd Division coming up from Dimapur had to fight their way through to link up with the 161st Indian Brigade at Jotsoma. A resting shed, constructed by a local official, marks the spot today. Its plaque includes a reference to Bunker Hill, the bunker-covered Japanese position along the road there. Once the 2nd Division had arrived at Zubza, some of its artillery guns were positioned in the fields just off the road, from where they had fired on the Kohima area.

Aerial view of the runway at Dimapur. Photo by Hemant Singh Katoch.

Dimapur Railway Station. Photo by Hemant Singh Katoch.

9. Dimapur

The road twists and turns as it makes its way down the hills towards Dimapur in the plains. It is a scenic drive through jungled mountains and the small villages that dot the road en route. In its last stretch before the checkpost for the hills at Chumukedima, the road passes through what war accounts call the Nichugard Pass. This is where the road, with a river alongside, passes through a narrow gorge; it offers a direct route through the mountains that overlook Dimapur. In the confusion at the beginning of the battle, this was one of the areas from where the British expected to defend against a Japanese attack on Dimapur. It was here that the Royal West Kents were initially being sent down from Kohima at the start of the battle, before they were rushed right back up.

Once you hit the plains, the temperature rises dramatically and the road becomes busier. If Dimapur was a major supply base for the Allies in 1944, the city is the business hub for Nagaland today. It is home to the state's sole airport and railway station. The former lies near the road a little outside the main city. Indeed, this is where the 161st Indian Brigade was flown in from Arakan in March, an action that would go on to save Kohima from Mutaguchi's army.

If one has the time to spare, you can make a quick stop at the Dimapur Railway Station. Not that there is anything to remind you of the war there today. And yet, as you stand on one of the overhead pedestrian bridges and watch the movements of passengers and trains at the station, it is worth remembering how this station played a key part in the war. At the time it was known as Manipur Road, a reference to it being the railhead for Manipur and to the road that wound its way from here to Imphal via Kohima. Passing through it is the railway line that Mutaguchi had hoped to cut, as it was used by the Americans to transport supplies towards the Dibrugarh–Ledo area for onward flights over the Hump to the Chinese. It was also at this station where thousands of soldiers disembarked as they made their way towards Kohima (such as those of the British 2nd Division) and beyond. As such, it was part of the experience of many Allied soldiers who came to this part of the world. Visiting it allows one to retrace their Second World War journey.

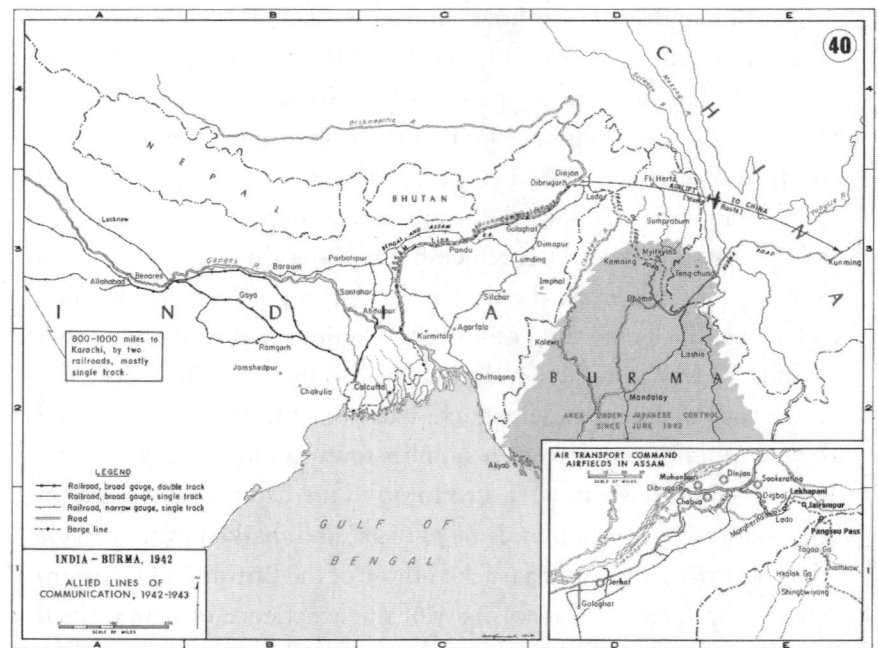

Allied lines of communication in India, Burma and China in 1942–43
Adapted from the original map by the Department of History, United States Military Academy

LEDO ROAD AND THE HUMP

Battle narrative

IF ONE HAD TO POINT out the most significant year of the Second World War in Northeast India, it would undoubtedly be 1944. All along and near the India–Burma frontier the most frenzied military activity took place, the likes of which the region had never seen before. The events of 1944 proved to be the turning point of the Burma Campaign, when advantage in this theatre of war slipped irrevocably to the Allies. Less than a year later, the Japanese had been comprehensively defeated in Burma.

Of course, it was around Imphal in Manipur and Kohima in the Naga Hills of Assam in 1944 that the maelstrom of the Second World War was well and truly felt in India, and where it reached its apogee. This area was the Burma Campaign's Central Front. But there was a lot going on further north as well. This had to do with American efforts to supply Chiang Kai-shek's forces who were fighting the Japanese in China. As noted earlier, in taking over Burma in 1942 the Japanese had succeeded in cutting the Allied supply line to the Chinese—the Burma Road. From then on, re-establishment of that supply line became the main priority in Burma for the Americans.

Since the main stretch of the Burma Road that ran through the country was firmly in Japanese hands, alternative ways and routes had to be found. Northern Burma and its vicinity (or the Northern Front) became the focus of the Americans. The immediate solution became the supply flights from Northeast India over the Eastern Himalayas to Kunming in China (the 'Hump' route). The longer-term solution became the construction of a new road from Ledo in eastern Assam through Northern Burma via the Pangsau Pass, to join up with the old Burma Road. This became known as the Ledo or Stilwell Road; the latter after US General Stilwell who commanded American forces in what they called the CBI theatre.

Therefore, in the year 1944 there was much action on the India–Burma frontier to the far north. Near the tea town of Dibrugarh, the air bridge to China over the Hump was operating at its peak. Thousands of sorties were being flown by the Americans to and from the airfields in Northeast India in some of the most dangerous flying conditions in the world. Allied planes were frequently crashing into the mountains of what is now Arunachal Pradesh, thanks to bad weather at extremely high altitudes. Soldiers from Chiang Kai-shek's army were carried back on many return flights from China, from where they were dispatched to Ramgarh in India (in Jharkhand today) for training by US personnel. They later formed X Force under Stilwell's command to fight the Japanese in Northern Burma.

At the same time, from other airfields in Northeast India, dozens of planes, many with gliders in tow, took off in March 1944. They were transporting men and materials for the second Chindit expedition, Operation Thursday, involving an entire division. They would be maintained from the air deep inside Japanese-held territory in Burma.

On the ground in 1944, with its starting point at Ledo, the Stilwell Road was being hacked through the jungles of Northern Burma. Involved in this endeavour were thousands of Americans and many more locals from both sides of the border. The road would finally be completed in January 1945. Also present would be tens of thousands of Chinese soldiers—X Force—who had set off from Ledo into Northern Burma. Their task was to support the opening of the land bridge to China by fighting the Japanese forces in the area.

In addition, deployed to the area was the American force that became popularly known as Merrill's Marauders. So named after their commander Frank Merrill, these were the only American ground troops in the CBI theatre, and they set off from Ledo in February

1944. They would subsequently play a major role in the capture of Myitkyina Airfield in Northern Burma.

Furiously ferrying supplies for the flights over the Hump and for the Allied military forces in the region were the locomotives of the Bengal and Assam Railway. From a peacetime tonnage of a few hundred tonnes a day, the trains on this route were now carrying thousands of tonnes. And finally, the mighty Brahmaputra River also played its part and was used for transporting materials that were too difficult or heavy to move by the existing roads and railways. It was a truly fascinating period in the entire region's history.

Battlefield guide

Dibrugarh in present-day Assam is the best jump-off point to explore the main Second World War sites in this part of Northeast India. From here you can easily access other areas in Upper Assam and continue on to present-day Arunachal Pradesh. This guide suggests a driving tour from Dibrugarh (or neighbouring Tinsukia) to Lekhapani via Digboi and Ledo—and back the same day. This requires no additional permits or permissions and makes for an interesting, if a little lengthy, day-long tour.

The runway at Mohanbari, the present-day Dibrugarh Airport.
Photo by Hemant Singh Katoch.

A tea picker at work alongside the Ledo/Stilwell Road between Jairampur and Pangsau, Arunachal Pradesh. Photo by Findlay Kember.

1. Dibrugarh and Chabua

Heading east from Dibrugarh, the road to Tinsukia runs parallel to a railway line, the two separated most of the way by mere metres. There are tea gardens on both sides in scenery that is typical for this part of Assam. It is a marked change from the combination of hills and paddy fields around Imphal and the soaring mountains at Kohima. The gardens remind one of the contribution of the Indian Tea Association during the Second World War. The tea industry was said to be the only source of organized labour in this part of India at the time. It provided assistance to the refugees who arrived from Burma in 1942 and thousands of its labourers were used to build airfields and roads in the region.

Carrying on down the road, you cross the town of Chabua; there are also turn-offs for Dibrugarh Airport (the old Mohanbari Airfield) and Dinjan. All three—Chabua, Mohanbari, Dinjan—are still home to airfields that first came up during the Second World War. There is also one at Doom Dooma (or the old Sookerating Airfield) that is beyond Tinsukia. These are among the collection of airfields that were carved out of the tea gardens for the flights over the Hump. Today almost all of them are closed off for civilians, except Mohanbari (and the abandoned Ledo Airfield. You can still spot them from a road nearby, although taking photographs of sensitive Indian defence installations is not permitted.

A caretaker cleaning gravestones at the Digboi War Cemetery. Photo by Findlay Kember.

A part of an oil pipeline that used to run alongside the Ledo/Stilwell Road during the Second World War. On display at the Digboi Centenary Museum. Photo by Hemant Singh Katoch.

An air raid shelter from the Second World War outside the Digboi Centenary Museum. Photo by Findlay Kember.

2. Digboi

From Dibrugarh you cross the markedly more commerce-oriented city of Tinsukia before heading towards the small oil town of Digboi. Digboi is considered the birthplace of the Indian oil industry. It was here that the British first discovered oil and the country's first oil refinery was set up. Parts of the town, especially where the offices and residences of personnel connected to the oil industry are located, therefore, have a distinctly colonial feel in their architecture and layout.

Digboi has two particular sites of interest. The first is the Digboi War Cemetery, the smallest of the five Second World War cemeteries maintained by the CWGC in Northeast India. The cemetery was started for burials from a military hospital that was established in the town during the war. Graves were later shifted here from other burial grounds in Assam nearby and from an American one in Burma. As with the others maintained by the CWGC, the Digboi War Cemetery is well looked after and now contains some 200 graves.

The second place to visit is the Digboi Centenary Museum. This excellent museum traces the discovery and growth of the oil industry in the area. Besides some information panels on the war, of particular interest is a section of pipe that is displayed within the museum's compound. This is part of the oil pipeline that was laid and ran along the Ledo/Stilwell Road during the Second World War. The pipe on display had been dug up and recovered. Another reminder of the war lies just outside the museum: an old air raid shelter. This dates back to 1942, a time when it was the Japanese who had supremacy in the skies above the India–Burma frontier, a situation that would be completely reversed as the war progressed.

The abandoned Ledo Airfield in Upper Assam.
Photo by Hemant Singh Katoch.

3. Ledo Airfield

From Digboi, you pass through the coal town of Margherita before arriving at Ledo. This small town in Assam lent its name to the famed road that was hacked through the jungle from here across Northern Burma: the Ledo/Stilwell Road. The construction of that road is the stuff of Second World War legend, but today Ledo is a quiet, nondescript Assamese town, with just the road signs bearing the town's name immediately resonating with anyone acquainted with the Burma Campaign.

What makes Ledo an interesting place to visit, however, is the abandoned airfield that sits on the outskirts of the town. Unlike the others around Dibrugarh and Tinsukia, here is an entire Second World War airfield that is yours to walk about and explore in splendid isolation. In fact, it is precisely the absence of official restrictions that makes Ledo Airfield such a joy to discover. This was the most forward of the airstrips that came up during the war and today you can freely walk its entire length.

A map showing the route of the Ledo/Stilwell Road at Stilwell Park, Lekhapani. Photo by Hemant Singh Katoch.

Zero Point, the starting point of the old Ledo/Stilwell Road. Photo by Hemant Singh Katoch.

4. Zero Point

Just beyond Ledo at Lekhapani is Zero Point, the starting point of the Ledo/Stilwell Road. Unlike many of the Second World War sites in Northeast India, this one is clearly marked, its significance highlighted by the Stilwell Park just off the road. This has an information panel about the road, as well as a large mounted map showing its trajectory and the distances to various places en route.

This part of the road today is asphalted and in a decent condition. But back in the war, those involved in constructing the road, including thousands of—mainly Black—Americans, had to find a way through the jungles, rivers and mountains of what was at the time eastern Assam and Northern Burma. Ironically, given the emphasis on the construction of the Ledo/Stilwell Road at the time, it did not prove to be the most efficient way of transporting supplies to China. The tonnage levels of supplies which the Allies were able to move along the road never approached those which were transported by aircraft over the Hump. For instance, in June 1945, just under 7,000 tonnes of supplies were transported using the Ledo/Stilwell Road, compared to around 70,000 tonnes that were flown over the Hump.

The last standing Chinese gravestone at an abandoned and overgrown cemetery near Lekhapani. Photo by Hemant Singh Katoch.

Lekhapani Railway Station. Photo by Hemant Singh Katoch.

5. Lekhapani Railway Station

After Zero Point is Lekhapani railway station, the easternmost point on the old Bengal and Assam Railway. This stretch of the old railway line runs along the road. The railway station itself lies abandoned today. Train services to the station ceased in the 1990s and it is now no longer in use; parts of the line from Ledo to Lekhapani have also gone to seed and some of the bridges in between have collapsed.

The old Lekhapani railway station is an atmospheric place to visit. There is a touch of melancholy about the station and its present state of abandonment—it makes you reflect on the incredible Second World War history of this part of India, and how for the most part it is forgotten today. Fortunately, in the case of this station, there is a neatly maintained stone marker nearby that sheds some light on its history as once being the station farthest east in India. Across the top of it is quite the appropriate heading: 'Railway's Last Frontier'.

Not quite as fortunate is an old cemetery, dating back to the war, near Lekhapani. The remains of the cemetery, which is again along the road, have been swallowed up by vegetation and there is little left to identify its graves. There used to be a couple of tombstones with Chinese inscriptions that were lying about in the bushes, but even those are difficult to locate today. The state of this site and its virtual disappearance serves as a reminder of the importance of preserving and promoting the Second World War-related sites of Northeast India.

Stone marker noting the history of the Lekhapani Railway Station. Photo by Findlay Kember.

A bridge on the abandoned stretch of the railway line near Lekhapani. Photo by Findlay Kember.

Guwahati

Guwahati War Cemetery. Photo by Hemant Singh Katoch.

Brahmaputra river at Guwahati. Photo by Hemant Singh Katoch.

The most economically dynamic and well-connected city in Northeast India today is Guwahati. Should you pass through it, the main Second World War site to visit is its war cemetery. This is the fifth Second World War cemetery in the region maintained by the CWGC. It is home to 486 Commonwealth burials of the war, of those who were brought from the military hospitals in the vicinity; several graves were also transferred here from isolated cemeteries in the region. As with the other CWGC cemeteries, this remains an oasis of calm and beauty in an otherwise busy city today.

6. Arunachal Pradesh: Jairampur, Pangsau Pass and Pasighat

Second World War cemetery near Jairampur, Arunachal Pradesh, along the Ledo/Stilwell Road. Photo by Findlay Kember.

A statue of a Chinese soldier stands in the war cemetery near Jairampur. Photo by Findlay Kember.

From Lekhapani in Assam, you can continue on up what was the old Ledo/Stilwell Road all the way to the Pangsau Pass at the India–Burma frontier. This involves crossing into and traversing the border state of Arunachal Pradesh, which has some restrictions on the entry of both foreign and Indian visitors (see 'Permits under Practical Information' section below).

Assuming that you have the required permits, the drive to the Burma border is a scenic one, besides being steeped in Second World

War history. For one, you are reminded of the fact that the road was hacked through the jungle: on some stretches even today, although the road is asphalted, the jungle closes on both sides and you start to get a sense of what it must have been like along its length at the time of the war.

By far the most interesting site en route is the old Second World War cemetery just beyond Jairampur. The story goes that this cemetery had been forgotten after the war and taken over by the surrounding jungle. It was discovered again only in the late 1990s. Since then, at least some effort has been made to try and secure the site. Today there is something by way of a compound wall, as well as signage and a sculpture of a soldier outside. A monument has been erected inside and it is dedicated to the men who lost their lives in the construction of the Ledo/Stilwell Road—an act, it notes, that was once thought to be an 'impossible engineering pipe dream'.

Engravings on a tomb illuminated by early morning sunlight in the cemetery near Jairampur. Photo by Findlay Kember.

Graves at the cemetery near Jairampur.
Photo by Findlay Kember.

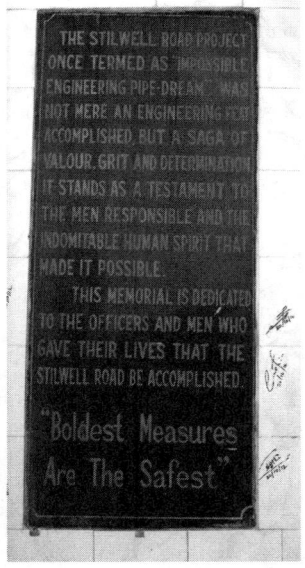

Inscription on memorial at the war cemetery, Jairampur.
Photo by Findlay Kember.

The Allied graves in the cemetery, which include those of the Chinese and locals from both sides of the border, are not in the best shape, however. The most prominent one seems to be that of a

Chinese, which has been marked out with a signboard that identifies him as Major Hsiao Chu Ching, the commander of '2nd Company, 2nd Battalion of 10th Regiment, Independent Engineers of Chinese Army stationed in India'. Some of the other graves are crumbling, while many are overgrown with moss and bushes.

From Jairampur you continue on the road and complete some border formalities at the last settlement on the Indian side, Nampong. The road makes its final ascent here over the Patkai Range before you reach the top of the range to the famed Pangsau Pass. From there you can see Burma on the other side. The Pangsau Pass is the main crossing-over point from Northeast India to Northern Burma, which the Ledo/Stilwell Road traverses. Before the road was constructed, this was also another escape route for thousands of refugees fleeing Burma at the time of the Japanese takeover of the country in 1942. The mountainous terrain and jungle on both sides had made this an especially difficult ordeal for the refugees.

An elephant and a mahout journey along the Ledo/Stilwell Road between Jairampur and Pangsau, Arunachal Pradesh.
Photo by Findlay Kember.

Vitrines at The Hump WWII Museum in Pasighat display artefacts retrieved from transport planes that crashed in the eastern Himalayas in the 1940s. Photo by Kai Friese.

Pangsau Pass, the main crossing over point between Northern Burma and Northeast India.
Photo by Findlay Kember.

From certain points around the Pangsau Pass today you can also catch a glimpse of the so-called Lake of No Return in the distance on the Burmese side. It is claimed that several planes crashed into this body of water during the Second World War.

On a related note, the mountains of Arunachal Pradesh are also the final resting place of hundreds of Americans who remain unaccounted for in plane crashes on the Hump route. The remains of some of these planes and their crews continue to be discovered in remote and relatively inaccessible areas. On its part, the US government is actively involved in trying to trace and retrieve the remains of its personnel who died while performing their war duty. A museum focused on the Hump route—The Hump WWII Museum—has recently been established in Pasighat. It exhibits the remains of several aircraft that were lost in the area and other artefacts related to the Hump operation.

5

Practical Information for Visitors

NORTHEAST INDIA IS TODAY MORE accessible for both domestic and foreign tourists than ever before. The overall trend in the region is of improved security, fewer travel restrictions, better connectivity and more comfortable accommodation options.

Security situation

For years the main news from large parts of Northeast India was dominated by scenes of violence, rebellion and the Indian security forces' operations. The security situation has stabilized greatly in recent times although there continue to be sporadic and localized incidents of unrest. Foreign nationals should, of course, refer to their respective governments' travel advisories, but the key point to take away is that compared to previous years, it is now much safer to travel in the region.

Permits

The Government of India has relaxed the system of permits that used to earlier restrict travel to the places covered in this battlefield guide. At the time of writing, foreign nationals no longer need to apply for a separate Protected Area Permit to visit Manipur or Nagaland; no special permits were required at the time of writing for the Dibrugarh–Ledo–Lekhapani area in Assam either. In the case of Manipur and Nagaland, any foreign national can visit them on their regular tourist visa. They only need to register themselves with the state authorities at the point of entry; a special desk for this has been set up at the land border in the case of Manipur and at Imphal and Dimapur Airports.

Indians from other states need to get an Inner Line Permit (ILP) to visit Nagaland and, as of January 2020, also to visit Manipur. All visitors to Arunachal Pradesh need permits, however. Indians need the ILP, while foreign nationals need to apply for a Protected Area Permit either at Indian missions abroad or at designated sites in India.

Transport links

Transport links to Northeast India have grown manifold in recent years, especially via airplanes. Guwahati is the best connected, with multiple daily flights to the main metropolitan cities in the country. Imphal is also now serviced by several daily flights from New Delhi and Kolkata, while Dibrugarh and especially Dimapur have fewer connections. You can also travel to Guwahati, Dimapur and Dibrugarh by train. All of the sites mentioned in this battlefield guide can be accessed by road, although road conditions in the hills of Manipur and Nagaland are not always the best.

For battlefield tours to Imphal and Kohima, you have the option of flying in to Imphal, driving up to Kohima, and then driving down to Dimapur to catch a flight (or train) out. That is the routing this battlefield guide has been structured on. Or you can do it the other way round: flying in to Dimapur and then driving to Imphal via Kohima. The thing to remember is that Imphal offers the best and cheapest options by air.

Accommodation

There was a time when hotels in Imphal and Kohima were limited and often confined to dimly lit and musty options in the main bazaar areas. Fortunately, this situation has changed too, and for the better. For Imphal and Manipur, the Classic Group of hotels is the best option. Their well-run properties in Imphal (and one in Moirang) are the most reliable for accommodation, although new hotels continue to open in the area. In Kohima, Hotel Vivor and De Oriental Grand are the preferred hotels, while the family-run heritage cottage of Razhu Pru is also an attractive option. In the Dibrugarh area you can go with the heritage tea bungalows run by Purvi Discovery.

Best season to visit

It is generally advised that any season other than the monsoon from May to August is a good time to visit. The period from October to March is probably the best time because it is cooler and drier then. Imphal and Kohima (in particular) can be surprisingly chilly in the winter months and visitors should carry sufficiently warm clothes with them. You can expect to tramp around the occasional hill or field during a battlefield tour, therefore, comfortable and appropriate footwear for the outdoors is recommended.

Tour operators

The Battle of Imphal Tours (www.battleofimphal.com) was created by the author in 2013. This pioneered and offered the first such Second

World War battlefield tours around Imphal and Kohima. These tours have since been successfully run and managed by Yaiphaba Meetei Kangjam ('Yai') based in Imphal and are available through the year. He has extensively researched the battles and the wider Burma Campaign. He also serves as the principal battlefield guide during the tours which have safely and expertly taken several hundred—mainly foreign—visitors around to these Second World War battlefields in Northeast India and Burma over the years. The Battle of Imphal Tours can be contacted via email on battleofimphal@gmail.com

Acknowledgements

I WOULD FIRST LIKE TO thank Sqn Ldr Rana Chhina at the United Service Institution of India's (USI) Centre for Armed Forces Historical Research (CAFHR) for encouraging me to write—and complete—this battlefield guide. Thanks are also due to Findlay Kember for taking and agreeing to share his evocative photos of these Second World War sites, gathered through his many visits to the region over the years. I am grateful to the Kohima Educational Trust for allowing the use of their excellent battlefield map of Kohima in this book. For the Imphal maps, a debt of gratitude is owed to two people: Robin Wahengam deserves recognition for transforming what was my original sketch into a beautiful map that has been used widely; and Hemam Bishwajeet Singh is to be lauded for being endlessly patient while continually improving this map over time. Finally, I am ever indebted to Yaiphaba Meetei Kangjam for all his help with this book and, more importantly, for doggedly persevering with, enhancing, and taking forward the battlefield tours of Northeast India and Myanmar (as part of the Battle of Imphal Tours) since their creation.

Bibliography

Allen, Louis. *Burma: The Longest War*. London: Phoenix Giant, 1984.

Bayly, Christopher and Tim Harper. *Forgotten Armies: Britain's Asian Empire and the War with Japan*. London: Penguin Books, 2005.

Brett-James, Antony. *Ball of Fire: The Fifth Indian Division in the Second World War*. Aldershot: Gale & Polden, 1951.

Brett-James, Antony and Geoffrey Evans. *Imphal, A Flower on Lofty Heights*. London: Macmillan, 1962.

Fay, Peter Ward. *The Forgotten Army*. Ann Arbor: University of Michigan Press, 1993.

Fraser, George MacDonald. *Quartered Safe Out Here: A Harrowing Tale of World War II*. New York: Akadine Press, 2001.

Freer, Arthur F. *Nunshigum*. Durham: The Pentland Press, 1995.

Grant, Ian Lyall. *Burma: The Turning Point*. Barnsley: Leo Cooper, 2003.

Hudson, John. *Sunset in the East*. Barnsley: Pen and Sword, 2002.

Keane, Fergal. *Road of Bones*. London: HarperCollins, 2011.

Kirby, S. Woodburn. *The War Against Japan*. Vol. 3. Uckfield: The Naval & Military Press, 1961.

Latimer, John. *Burma, The Forgotten War*. London: John Murray, 2004.

Lyman, Robert. *Kohima 1944*. Oxford: Osprey Publishing, 2010.

Molloy, Terence R. *The Silchar Track*. Ely: Melrose Books, 2006.

Nunnely, John and Kazuo Tamayama. *Tales by Japanese Soldiers*. London: Cassell & Co., 2000.

Prasad, Bisheshwar, ed. *Official History of the Indian Armed Forces in the Second World War: 1939–45—The Reconquest of Burma*. 2 vols. New Delhi: Pentagon Press, 2014. (Originally published in 1958.)

Seaman, Harry. *The Battle at Sangshak*. London: Leo Cooper, 1989.

Swinson, Arthur. *Kohima*. London: Cassell, 1966.

Thompson, Julian. *Forgotten Voices of Burma*. UK: Ebury Press, 2009.

Toye, Hugh. *Subhash Chandra Bose: The Springing Tiger*. Mumbai: Jaico Publishing House, 1991.

———. *Japan's Last Bid for Victory*. Barnsley: Praetorian Press, 2011.

Slim, William J. *Defeat into Victory*. London: Cassell, 1956.

United States Army. *Burma Operations Record: 15th Army Operations in Imphal Area and Withdrawal to Northern Burma*. Japan, 1957.

Online sources

Supplement to the *London Gazette*, 10 October 1944. https://www.thegazette.co.uk/London/issue/36742/supplement/4673

Supplement to the *London Gazette*, 12 December 1944. https://www.thegazette.co.uk/London/issue/36833/supplement/5673/data.pdf

Index*

Advance Ordnance Depot, 121–122
African countries, 13
airfields, 6, 54, 79, 84–86, 117, 172–173; Allies and, 7; Dibrugarh Airport—Mohanbari, 7–8, 12; Doom Dooma (or old Sookerating Airfield), 173; Imphal Valley, 40, 43, 116; in Manipur, 54; in Northeast India, 7, 170; Palel, 83; Sapam, 83
Allies/Allied, 1–3, 7, 41, 167, 169, 177; in Burma theatre of war, 10; lines of communication *168*; military forces, 8, 13, 171; planes, 12, 170
American: B-25 Mitchell bomber, 117; Field Service, 12
Americans, 6–8, 16, 54, 167, 169–170, 174, 185, (*see also* Black-Americans); Hump route to China, 12
Aradura Spur, 37–38, 131–132, 134, 136, 142, 149–152, 155, 157; old *148*
Arakan, 6, 10, 15–16, 18, 24–26, 34, 96–97, 114, 117, 130–131, 167
Arakan operation, 17
artillery, 20–27, 29–31, 56, 76, 88, 90, 99, 102–103, 120, 163
Arunachal Pradesh, 2, 4, 170, 181, 184–185, 188; tea picker *172*
Assam, 2, 4, 7, 41, 52, 117, 152, 156, 169, 172, 174; old Barracks area, 157

---

* Page numbers in bold italic face denote images.

Assam Regiment, 25, 34, 111–112, 130, 156; 1st, 25, 34, 111–112, 130; memorial to *155*

Assam Rifles ('Dhai Murty'), 21, 84, 88, 108, 130, 142, 156–157; Garrison Hill, 142–145; memorials to *141*, *155*

Bangladesh, 12

Battalion of Royal West Kents (161st Indian Brigade), 35

Battle of Imphal Tours (www.battleofimphal.com), 189

Battle at Jessami, 34

Battle at Kharasom, 34

battlefields, 45, 54–55, 57, 73, 87, 107, 115, 117–118, 133–134, 142, 144, 146, 149, 156–157; tours, 188–189, 191; guides, 44, 52, 54, 82, 97, 115, 133, 171, 188–191

Battle of Attrition, 51

Battle of Burma, 129

Battle of Imphal *42*; Tours, 189–191

battleofimphal@gmail.com, 190

Battle of the Admin Box, Japanese defeat in, 18

Bishenpur (Bishnupur), 37, 52–53, 55, 59–63, 67, 70–72

Black—Americans, 177

Black Cats, 52–53, 60, 62; of 17th Indian Division, 51

bombing, 48, 117

Bose, Subhas Chandra, 11, 19, 69

Bower, Ursula Graham, 9

Brahmaputra River 2, 4, 171, *180*

Brahmaputra Valley, 1, 18, 129

Brett-James, Antony, 80

Briggs, Maj. Gen. 114

British/Britons, 90, 107, 133

British Army, 131; Fourteenth Army, 8, 12, 14–20, 40–41, 43, 47, 51, 53, 96–97, 107, 109, 125–126, 130, 147; Fifteenth Army, 11–12, 17–19, 29, 40, 44; ; in Burma (Burma Corps), 4; forces, 15–16, 41, 43, 56, 64, 71, 104, 122, 131, 159; Jungle warfare, 15; loss of tank officers, 100; retreat abandoning DIS Hill on Kohima, 35; 2nd Division, 34, 40–41, 124–126, 131–132, 139, 145, 147–148, 155, 159–160, 163, 165, 167;

Bunker Hill, 165; marker at **164**
Burma, 1–19, 41, 51–52, 54, 65, 80, 86–87, 93, 95, 97, 112, 114, 140, 156–157, 168–170; Burma. anti-Indian riots, 3; Chinese forces escape through, 4; fall of, 3; Northern, 6, 8, 12, 169–171, 175, 177, 184, 194
Burma Area Army, 17, 29, 41
Burma Campaign, 2, 12, 113, 148, 169, 175, 190
Burma Corps, 4, 15
Burma Road, 4, 6, 8, 169; to Chiang Kai-shek, 3
Burma theatre of war, Allies in, 10

casualties, 12, 41, 44, 52, 77, 151
cemeteries, 13, 44, 47, 137, 146–149, 174, 178, 182; Allied graves in, 183
Chiang Kai-shek, 3–4, 6, 169–170
China–Burma–India (CBI), 8
Chindit expedition, 54, 170
Chindit operation (Chindits/Operation Longcloth/Long Range Penetration Brigade), 10–11, 17, 27, 109, 117, 157
Chinese soldiers, 4, 12, 170; gravestone near Lakhpani **177**; at war cemetery **181**
Chin Hills, 51
Chumukedima, 160, 166
Classic Group of hotels, 189, *see also* hotels
Commonwealth soldiers, 47, 146
Commonwealth War Graves Commission (CWGC), 13, 47, 147, 174, 180; cemeteries, 13, 146, 180; Imphal Indian
Cowan, Punch, Maj. Gen., 2ll, 51, 56; *See also* Black Cats
Craddock, Sq. Ser. Maj., 100
Cremation Memorials, 47, 49, 146
Crete, 36, 80, 87, 89
Cross of Sacrifice, 148
Cyprus, 80, 89

Dakota, 28–29, 117
Detail Issue Store (DIS), 136, 139–140, 143
Devonshire Regiment, 1st, 22, 88

Dibrugarh Airport (old Mohanbari Airfield), 7, *171*–172
Dibrugarh in present-day Assam, 7–8, 12, 129, 167, 170–172, 174–175, 188
Dibrugarh–Ledo–Lekhapani area, 188
Digboi, 171, 175; Centenary Museum, *174*; War Cemetery *173*–174
Dimapur, 7–8, 11, 113, 117, 126–127, 129–131, 134, 136–137, 145, 159–160, 163, 166–167, 188–189; runway at *165*
Dimapur Airports, 188
Dimapur–Kohima–Imphal Road, 40
Dimapur Railway Station *166*–167
Dinjan, 172
Dogras, 99–100, 102, 125
Dome 73, *78*
Doom Dooma (old Sookerating Airfield), 173
Dyer Hill, Pimple and Big Tree Hill, *159*

Eastern Army, 8, 14
Eastern Himalayas, 7, 119, 169, 185

Evans, Geoffrey, 60

Field Supply Depot (FSD), 136, 139–140, 143
Finch Corner, 104–106; stone marker for, *104*
First World War, 90
foliage, 62–63, 72
Fraser, George MacDonald, 43

G
Gagiphe: memorial at *162*–163; trek up to, 163
Ganju Lama, Rifleman, 38
Garrison Hill (or Summerhouse Hill), 136–137, 142–144
Garrison Memorial, *139*
General Purpose Transport (GPT) Ridge, 134
Geoffrey Evans, 193
George Hill *123*
Gibraltar, 37, 80, 85, 87, 91, 93, 133; Japanese positions on, 92
GPT Ridge 37, 142–143, 149, 151–*152*
Gracey, Douglas Maj. Gen., 81, 131, 157, 163
Grover, John M.L. 131, 157, 163; Memorial, *162*
Gun Spur, 157
Gurkha Rifles, 4/1st, 27, 140

Gurkhas, 40, 80, 82, 84, 90–92, 107, 133; from Nepal, 12
Guwahati, 180, 188; War Cemetery, **180**

Hafiz, Jemadar Abdul, 35, 101
Hand-to-hand fighting, 72, 108
Harman, John, Lan. Corp., 35, 143
Harry Hill **123**
The Heritage, 142–143
The heritage tea bungalows, by Purvi Discovery, 189, *see also* hotels
Hindu soldiers, 47, 146
Honda Raiding Unit (15th Division), 127
Hope-Thomson, Brig., 96
Hornbill Festival, 161
hotels, 189, *see also* Classic Group of hotels; The heritage tea bungalows, by Purvi Discovery
Howrah Bridge, 123
Hsiao Chu Ching, Maj., 184
Hudson, John, 93
Hump, 7–8, 12, 118–119, 133, 167, 169–171, 173, 177, 186
The Hump WWII Museum, 186; Vitrines at, **185**

Hunters Hill, 157
Hurribombers, 88, 99, 117

Ikkenya, 81
Imperial General Headquarters, Tokyo, 11
Imperial Japanese Army, 18
Imphal, battle, 53–54, 57–58, 60, 71, 73, 81, 83, 90–92, 96, 104, 115; battlefields of, 45; battle point, 120; Japanese strongholds, 126; Japanese withdrawal from, 38
Imphal Airport, 188
Imphal–Dimapur road, 136
Imphal Indian Army War Cemetery, Cremation Memorial, **49**
Imphal–Kohima–Dimapur Road, 17, 70, 95, 113, 137–**138**; old DIS with **140**; stone marker at **160**
Imphal–Kohima Road, 35, 40, 45, 49, 71, 94, 97, 113–127, 160; Honda Raiding Unit at, 34; old bridge on, **126**
Imphal Main, 48, 83, 117–119
Imphal Main Airfield (or Koirengei Airfield), 48, 99,

115; 'Air Battle of Imphal,' 116
Imphal Peace Museum, 58–***59***
Imphal *turel* (river) 120, 123–***124***, 127
Imphal Valley, 8, 11, 16, 35, 40, 43, 51–54, 80–81, 113, 116, 118; key Japanese position in, 64
Imphal War Cemetery ***46***–47; Africans in, 13
Imphal War Museum, 48; exhibits from ***49***
India and Burma, 1, 11, 80, 93; border, 14; frontier-mountains along 2, 4–***5***, 8, 10, 16, 44, 169–170, 175, 181; border, 86
Indian Army, 11, 27, 47, 84, 108, 116, 122
Indian Brigade, 21–25, 27, 34–37, 60, 63, 67, 114, 119, 130–131, 140, 152, 156, 159; 161st, 163, 167; Point 5846 off Silchar–Bishenpur Track, 36
Indian Division: 'hammer and anvil' strategy 67; 5th, 16, 24–25, 34, 36, 40, 96–97, 99, 114–115, 117–118, 124, 126, 130; 7th, 16, 24, 26, 131–132, 140; 17th, 17, 33–34, 51–53, 56, 59, 62–63, 96, 114; 20th, 16–17, 22, 35, 81, 88–89, 96–97, 103; 23rd, 16, 23, 33–34, 36, 52, 81, 91–92, 96–97, 102, 104
Indian General Hospital (IGH) Spur or Hospital Spur, 136, 143–144
Indian National Army (INA), 11–12, 18–29, 68–69, 71, 81, 84, 129; attack on Palel Airfield, 36; flag 68; Manipur headquarters Moirang, ***70***; Martyrs' Memorial, 69; Order of Battle, 32; as part of U-Go, 19; soldiers, 82–83
Indian National Army Memorial Complex, Moirang, ***68***
Indian Parachute Brigade, 50th, 23, 34, 56, 96, 106–107
Indians, 3, 15, 40, 43, 80–82, 90, 107, 122, 184, 188, 195; as refugees, exodus of, 3; from Southeast Asia, 12
Indian Tea Association in Assam, 4
India Peace Memorial, ***57***–58

Inner Line Permit (ILP), 188
Iril River Valley, 44–45, **94**–95, 97, 99–100, 113–114
Isaac Hill, **123**

Jail Hill, 35, 136–137, 143, 151–152
Jairampur, 172, 181, 183–184; Chinese buried at, 13; tomb cemetery near, **182**
James Hill, **123**
Japanese: and 7/10th Baluch Regiment, 56; 15th Division, 7, 17–19, 33, 39, 95, 102, 113, 147; 31st Division, 18–19, 33–35, 37, 95–96, 113, 129, 136; 33rd Division, 18, 51–52, 60, 69, 114; 51st Regiment attacks Nungshigum, 35; against the British defences, 53; approaching Imphal, 45; arrived at Kohima, 35, 130, 142; attacks on Bishenpur, 37; attacks on India, 7; attacks on Pearl Harbor, 3; attacks Sekmai, 35, 119; bunkers, 100, 151; capturing Rangoon, 3; casualties, 107; held Scraggy's crest, 91; invasion of Allied colonies, 3; in Malaya, 11; memorials, 13; in Singapore, 11; supply lines, 10, 117; takes over FSD Hill and Kuki Piquet, 36; taking Burma, 2–5, 10, 15, 17–18, 86, 170
Japanese Army Air Force, 31, 60
Japanese soldiers, 6, 54–55, 58, 61, 67, 73, 88, 110, 118, 163–164, 194; loss of, 80, 100, 102
Japanese war memorials, 56; Maibam village, **58**
Jat companies/Jats, 99, 101, 123–125
Jessami 34, **110**–111; Assam Regiment Memorial at, **112**
Jotsoma, 36, 132, 135, 145, 159, 163, 165; memorial for Japanese soldiers, **164**; Memorial in, **162**

Kabaw Valley in Burma, 13
Kakching Garrison, 84
Kakching Lamkhai, 85
Kameng, 101–103
Kangjam ('Yai'), Yaiphaba Meetei, 190
Kangla Airfield, fair-weather airfields, **98**–99

Kanglatongbi, 35, 119–122; as Lion Box, 35, 121–122; War Memorial, *121*–122

Kangpokpi, 34, 115, 126–127, 160; bridge, 126

Kasom, T.M., 104

Kawabe, 129

Kawamichi, 81

Kharasom, 111–112

Khurai Chingambam Mandap, Impha,, *5*, 48

Kiani, Zaman Mohammad, Col., 19

Kigwema, 160, 162

Kisama, 160, 162; Kigwema *160*0; siege of, 130, 136; World War II Museum in, *161*

Kohima, defenders of, 130; panorama of, *132*

Kohima battle, 40, 111, 113, 132, 143–144, 157, 163; second phase of, 40

Kohima battlefield, 133; locations, *128*; tour, 142

Kohima Cathedral, *149*, *150*, 152

Kohima Epitaph, 147–148

Kohima Ridge, 35–36, 40, 129, 131, 134–*135*, 136, 138, 143–145, 149, 152, *158*,

165; main, 157; old, 136–137, 142; recovered from Japanese 31st Division, 37

Kohima Road, 34–36, 38, 40, 44–45, 49, 71, 97, 114–116, 118, 123–124, 126

Kohima War Cemetery, 137, *146*–147; Cremation Memoria, *148*

Koirengei, 48, 118

Kuki Piquet, 36, 136, 139; old, 135, 138–139, 143

Kunming, 7, 169

Lake of No Return, 185

Lambui/Lamu or Lammu, 104

Lambui–Ramva area, 105

Lamdan, 73

Lamlai, 102–103

Ledo Airfield, 7, 11–12, 169–171, 173, *175*–176, 178, 188; old, *9*

Ledo or Stilwell Road, 9, 12, 169–186; elephant with mahout, *184*; Lekhapani, *176*; old, 181; old, Zero Point, *176*

Lee/Grant of the 3rd Carabiniers, 139

Lekhapani: Assam, 171, 177–179; as Zero Point, 176

Index

Lekhapani Railway Station, stone marker at, *179*
Lekhapani Railway Station, *177*–178
Litan, 102–104
Loktak Lake, 59, 69–*70*
London Bridge, 123

machine guns, 92, 103, 139, 143, 153
Maejima, 81
Maharaja of Manipur in Imphal, 4
Maibam, 55–56
Malta, 80, *85*, *89*, 91–93
Manipur, 2, 11–12, 15, 41, 44, 47–48, 51, 54, 59, 69, 117, 120, 167, 169, 188–189; battlefield tourism, 45; mountains, *5*
Manipur Rifles, 93
Manipur Tourism Forum, 59
Mapao–Molvom Range, 37, 45, 97, 113–115, *116*, 117–120, *121, 123*, 127
Masakazu, Kawabe, Lt. Gen. 17
Matsumura, Col., 29, 118
Meghalaya, 2
Merema, 134, 159
Merema Ridge, 131, *145*, 157, 159
Merrill, Frank, 12, 170

Milestone 109, 125–126
military hospitals, 174, 180
Miyazaki, Maj. Gen., 106
Mizoram, 2
Mohanbari, 7, 172–173; runway at, *171*
Moirang, 67–69, 189
Moreh, Manipur, 4, 35, 81–82, 87
Moreh Road, 82
Motbung, 118, 122–123
Mountbatten, Louis, Vice Adm. Lord, 14, 129
Mount Puliebadze (Pulie Badze), 134
Myitkyina Airfield in Northern Burma, 171

Naga Heritage Village, 161
Naga Hills of Assam, 129
Naga Hospital, 144
Nagaland, 2, 133, 137, 160, 167, 188; Raj Bhavan, 144
Nagaland Police headquarters, 151–*152*
Nagas, 9, 37, 163–164
Naga Village, 131, 134, 136, 140, 142, 145–146, 156
Nichugard Pass, 166
Ningthoukhong, 38, 62, 64–67, 73

Ningthoukhong Kha Khunou, 65
Nippon Foundation, 59
Nippon Hill, 87, **89**, 91, 93; old, 87; recaptured by Devons, 88
Norfolks, 155; memorial, 156
North East Inda, and foreign nationals, 187–188
Northeast India, 1–8, 10–13, 35, 41, 44, 169–171, 174, 176, 178, 180, 184–185, 190–191; Security situation in, 187; transforms, 6–9; transport link to, 188
Nungshigum, 36, 100–101, 118, 133; heights *98*; Japanese attack on, 99

old Naga Village (Kohima village), 144, 151, 156–159
Operation Stamina, 117
Operation Thursday, 170
Operation 'U-Go.' *See under* Renya, Mutaguchi
Order of Battle: British, 20–29; Japanese, 29–32

Palel/Pallel Airfield, 36, 80, 82–84, 86; INA attack on, 84; old, 84–**85**; all-weather airfield, 83

Pangsau Pass, 4, 169, 181, 184–185
Pasighat, 181, 186
Patkai Range, 184
Point 2926 (Red Hill), 37, **55**–57, 59–60, **78**, 85, 87, 93; trenches on **90**
Point 3404, 66–67
Point 3524, 103
Point 4057, 102
Point 4241, 102–103
Point 5846 (or Laimaton), 36, 63, 70–**74**, **78**
Point 7378, 106, 110
Potsangbam, 62–64, 67; 'Pots and Pans,' 61
Protected Area Permit, 188
Pulie Badze/Puliebadze, 134
Punjab Memorial, 140–**141**, 142–143
Punjab Regiment, 3/14th, 24, 119, 123; 3/2nd, 24, 130; 4/15th, 140

Queen's Own Cameron Highlanders: 1st, 26, 159; Memorial to, **158**

Rai, Naik Agan Singh, 63
Railway's Last Frontier, 178
Raj Bhavan, 137, 142
Rajputana Rifles, 23, 92

Randle, John Niel, Capt., 37, 151–153
Rangoon, 6, 41, 86
refugees, 3–4, 86, 172, 184; from Burma, 142; entered India, 4
Renya, Mutaguchi: Lieutenant General, 11, 17–19, 29, 43, 52–53, 95, 129, 167; army, 43, 167; Fifteenth Army of, 129; U-Go of, 18
RKCS Art Gallery, 48
Royal Air Force (RAF), 117
Royal Gurkha Rifles, 2/5th, 21, 63
Royal Norfolk Regiment, memorial to, *154*
Royal Norfolks, 151
Royal Scots, 26, 155–156; Memorial to, *154*
Royal West Kents, 4th, 35, 130, 143, 166
Runaway Hill, 35, *101*

Saddle, 80, 82–83, 86–87, 89, 92–93, 102–103; on Ukhrul Road, *103*; under Japanese control, 102
Sapam airfield, 83, 98, *see also* airfields
Saparmeina, 123–124

Sasakawa Peace Foundation, 59
Sato, Lt. Gen., 31, 37, 95, 129, 143, 149, 151, 162
Scoones, Geoffrey, Lt. Gen., 20
Scraggy, 88, *89*–92, 133; old battlefield, 87, 90
Second World War, 1–2, 7–8, 44–45, 47–48, 54, 64, 69–70, 86–87, 92–93, 105, 108, 115–116, 133, 135–136, 146–147, 172, 175, 181, 193–194; battlefield tours, 189–190; Burma Campaign of, 12; sites, 171, 176, 178, 180, 191; in Ukhrul, memorial or monument to, 110
Second World War cemetery, Jairampur *181*
Second World War Imphal Campaign Foundation, 59
Sekmai, 36, 118–120, 122
Shangshak/Sangshak, 34, 95–97, 102, 105–108, 112, 194; war memorial, *109*
Shangshak village: British defensive position at, *105*; trenches at, *106,* 107–*108*
Shenam Saddle or Shenam Pass, 33, 36–38, 45, 78, 79–83, 80, *85*–89, 91–93, 96, 104

Shokvao, 104
Sikh soldiers, 47, 146
Silchar, 44–45, 50, 60, 70, 74; Japanese blow up bridge on, 36
Silchar–Bishenpur Track (Silchar Track), 36, 38, 44–45, **50**–52, 74, **75**
Silchar Track, 35, 52–53, 60, 63–64, 70–72, 74, 114, 194
Singh, Arjan, Air Marshal, 117
Singh, Ranbir, Sub., 100
Slim, William J., Lt. Gen., 8, 39, 44–45, 47, 51, 53, 95, 113, 117; 11 corps under, 15; force, 18; 'hub and spoke' of, 44–45; as Viscount Field Marshal, 1, 15–16
Slim Cottage in Kangla Fort Complex, **46**–48
snipers, Japanese, 100
South East Asia Command (SEAC), 14, 20
Southern Bump (or Twin Bumps), 99
Spitfires, 28, 117
Stilwell, Joe, American General, 4
Stilwell Road, 7, 12, 169–170
Stopford, M. Gen., 16, 130

strafing, 100, 117, 119

Tamu–Palel Road, 5, 17–18, 33, 35, 44–45, 51, 79–**85**, 86, 93, 95
Thapa, Netra Bahadur, Sub. VC citation for, 5, 16–18, 33, 35, 37, 44–45, 51, 63, 75–77, 79–86, 93, 95
Tiddim Road, 17–18, 33–35, 37–38, 44–45, **50**, 51–**55**, 57, 59–**61**, 62–65, 67, 73, 82, 95–96
Tinsukia, 172–175
Torbung Roadblock, 37, 67
tour operators, 189–190
trek, 73, 163
Tripura, 2
Tulihal Airfield (Bir Tikendrajit International Airport), 54
Turner, Hanson Victor, Ser, 38, 65
twin battles, 1, 39, 97, 126, 160

Ukhrul region, 38, 95–96, 104–106, 109–110, 157
Ukhrul Road, 36–37, 44–45, **94**–99, **101**–103, 105, 113
Ukhrul–Shangshak area, 97
Ukhrul town, **109–110**

Index

U.S. Troop Carrier Command, 117

Vengeance dive bombers, 99, 117
V Force, intelligence of British, 9
Victoria Crosses, 41, 53, 63, 65, 72, 101, 143, 151
'Vinegar Joe' Stilwell, 7–8

Wangjing Airfield, 82–83, 98
war cemetery, 142, 146, 180–181; Jairampur, **183**; old Second World, 182
Warren, Brigadier, 156
Wavell, Viceroy, 117
West Hill position, old, 107
West Kents, 130–131
West Yorkshires, 2nd, 65, 123
White Tigers, 51–53, 60, 67
Wingate, Orde, Maj. Gen., 10, 117: death of, 34
Wireless Hill (Antenna to the Japanese), 71, 73, **78**

Wooded Hill, 73
Wooded Ridge (or Mori to Japanese), 78
'Woodforce,' recovered Red Hill and Maibam, 56
World War II Museum, Kisama, 161

X Force, 12

Yamamoto, Maj. Gen., 81
Yamamoto Force, 36–37, 81–83, 88–89, 91; captures Crete East and Cyprus, 36; captures Gibraltar, 37; occupies Scraggy, 37; recaptures Nippon Hill, 36
Yamauchi, Lt. Gen., 95–96, 106, 113–115, 119, 122
Yanagida, Lt. Gen., 51, 96

Zubza, 131, 134, 145, 159, 164–165

Other Books in the Series

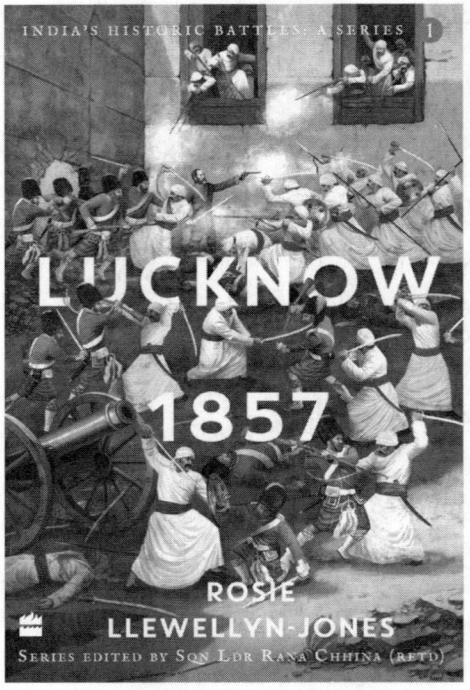

The city of Lucknow was the epicentre of the uprising of 1857.

In *Lucknow, 1857*—part of a new series of books on India's historic battles—historian Rosie Llewellyn-Jones examines the conflict in detail, from the British annexation of Awadh to the Indian response and the subsequent revolt by sepoys. The defeat of a unit of the East India Company's army at Chinhat led immediately to the siege of the extensive British Residency in the heart of the city. Here, nearly 3,000 people—British, Indian and Anglo-Indian—held out for four and a half months. The winter saw huge defensive barricades being built around Lucknow, but with their superior firepower, the British recapture was the inevitable outcome.

This richly illustrated field guide draws on Llewellyn-Jones's intimate knowledge of the city to paint a vivid picture of the events that unfolded in this historic urban battlefield.

Other Books in the Series

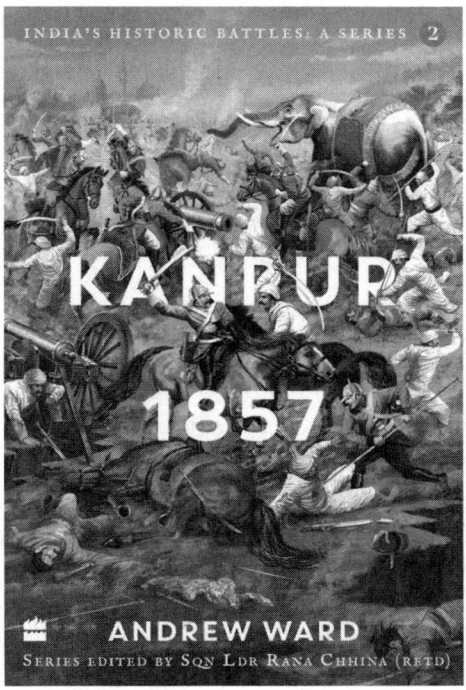

Of all the horrors that blackened the uprising of 1857, none could match the atrocities committed at Kanpur.

In *Kanpur, 1857*—part of a new series of books on India's historic battles—historian Andrew Ward gives an unblinking account of the siege of the entrenchment into which the European community fled when the town's four native regiments rebelled, the massacre at the Sati Chaura Ghat, and the hacking to death of the surviving Europeans. Their slaughter would exacerbate the savage and indiscriminate killings the British were already carrying out, burning villages and condemning thousands of locals to flogging, degradation and the gallows.

This richly illustrated field guide draws on decades of research to depict the pitched battles, and the acts of heroism and sacrifice on both sides that were subsumed by campaigns of atrocity and terror.

About the United Service Institution of India

ESTABLISHED IN 1870 BY MAJOR General Sir Charles MacGregor in Shimla (then Simla), the United Service Institution of India (USI) is a national security and defence services think tank based in New Delhi. Its aim is the 'furtherance of interest and knowledge in the art, science and literature of the defence services'. It is located at Vasant Vihar, New Delhi, from where it has been operating since 1996.

About the Centre for Military History and Conflict Studies
(Formerly Centre for Armed Forces Historical Research)

THE CENTRE WAS ESTABLISHED IN December 2000 under the aegis of the USI for encouraging the objective study of all facets of Indian military history with a special emphasis on the history of the Indian Armed Forces. It focuses on diverse aspects of the history of Indian military evolution, policies and practices—strategic, tactical, logistical, organisational and socio-economic, as well as the field of contemporary conflict studies.

About the Author

Hemant Singh Katoch is an independent scholar and consultant based in New Delhi. His research has focused on the battles of Imphal and Kohima of 1944 and he has pioneered battlefield tours around them. He has also worked for several years for the Centre for Humanitarian Dialogue in Switzerland and Myanmar. He has had stints with the United Nations World Food Programme in Timor-Leste and with the International Committee of the Red Cross in the Democratic Republic of Congo.

HarperCollins *Publishers* India

At HarperCollins India, we believe in telling the best stories and finding the widest readership for our books in every format possible. We started publishing in 1992; a great deal has changed since then, but what has remained constant is the passion with which our authors write their books, the love with which readers receive them, and the sheer joy and excitement that we as publishers feel in being a part of the publishing process.

Over the years, we've had the pleasure of publishing some of the finest writing from the subcontinent and around the world, including several award-winning titles and some of the biggest bestsellers in India's publishing history. But nothing has meant more to us than the fact that millions of people have read the books we published, and that somewhere, a book of ours might have made a difference.

As we look to the future, we go back to that one word— a word which has been a driving force for us all these years.

Read.